Indian Pandemic Law : A Deep Dive Into COVID-19's Legal Impact

Dr. Deepti Meena

Indian Pandemic Law : A Deep Dive into COVID-19's Legal Impact

Indian Pandemic Law : A Deep Dive into COVID-19's Legal Impact

Dr. Deepti Meena

ASSOCIATED
PUBLISHING HOUSE

Edition - 2023

ISBN: 978-81-965309-9-0

Published by:
Associated Publishing House
Block No. 77, Sanjay Place, Agra.

Preface

In the pages that follow, you will embark on a journey of knowledge, exploration, and discovery. This book is the culmination of countless hours of research, contemplation, and dedication, and it is with great pleasure that I present it to you.

As the author, I want to express my deepest gratitude to those who have supported and inspired me throughout this endeavor. Writing a book is no solitary task; it is the result of a collective effort.

First and foremost, I owe my sincerest thanks to my father, Mr. G.R. Meena, whose wisdom and guidance have been a source of inspiration throughout my life. His unwavering support has been a guiding light on this journey.

To my mother, Mrs. Krishna Meena, I am deeply grateful for your boundless love and encouragement. Your unwavering faith in my abilities has been a constant source of motivation.

My husband, Mr. Arun Meena, has been my rock and my greatest supporter. His patience, understanding, and belief in my work have been the cornerstones of my success. I couldn't have asked for a better partner in life and in this creative endeavor.

I also want to express my heartfelt thanks to my father-in-law, Mr. Ram Prasad Meena, and my mother-in-law, Mrs. Kamala Meena. Their unwavering support, love, and encouragement have been a tremendous source of strength and motivation.

To my entire family, thank you for being a source of inspiration and for always cheering me on. Your support means the world to me.

I also wish to acknowledge the invaluable guidance and mentorship I received from Dr. Abhishek Baplawat, whose expertise and wisdom have enriched the content of this book. Their insights have been instrumental in shaping the ideas presented within these pages.

This book is a testament to the power of collaboration, curiosity, and the pursuit of knowledge. It is my hope that it will inspire, inform, and ignite the same passion for learning in you, the reader, that it has in me. As you embark on this literary journey, I encourage you to approach each chapter with an open mind and a sense of wonder.

Thank you for choosing to explore the world of ideas and insights within these pages. May this book enrich your mind and deepen your understanding of the subject matter. Your engagement with its contents is the greatest honor an author can receive.

Warmest regards

Dr. Deepti Meena

CONTENTS

01
CHAPTER

INTRODUCTION

1.1 Introduction

1.1.1 Background

Given the underlying reality that the changing requirements and circumstances, the present thesis is of highest significance to the research scholar. Public health laws have been amended in accordance with the Law of Social Transformation, which has always highlighted that laws are modified in response to shifts in society's requirements. Therefore, how society's needs change drives changes in the law. It is also an initiative to identify and highlight the public health rules, regulations, legislative imperatives and standards of health concerns that have evolved over time as a result of numerous epidemic or pandemic diseases that have struck the entire world with their impact on India. One such disease that has recently gained attention is COVID-19, for which it was determined that the most significant international and national health laws, legislations, rules, and regulations needed to be amended. Therefore, present thesis goes into an in-depth analysis of COVID-19 pandemic taking an insight from all the previous such cases that have struck the world to study its impact on Public Health laws.

1.1.2 Concept and Terminology

Before beginning with the thesis, it is important to elaborate the key concepts from where the entire conceptual basis of the present thesis has developed. The major terms to be confronted again and again in the thesis as well as being dealt with today since 2019 are – Pandemic, Epidemic, Endemic, and COVID-19.

Pandemic

Many people used the phrases "pandemic" or "epidemic" to describe the spread of disease throughout the 17th and 18th centuries. As early as 1666, the term "pandemic" was used to describe "an endemic, or vernacular illness" that "always reigned in a Country". When Noah Webster published his first edition of Webster's Dictionary[1] in 1828, he included epidemic and pandemic as synonyms for the first time. The term "epidemic," when used as a "noun," had therefore become the standard phrase for what we still refer to as "epidemic" and "pandemic," with the overused term "pandemic" becoming more and more common.[2] The scientific knowledge of how illnesses spread has also evolved along with society and certain contemporary definitions encompass "extensively epidemic, "epidemic... across a very vast area and generally affecting a substantial percentage of the population," as well as "widely spread or occurring across a region, country, continent, or the world". The novel coronavirus pandemic serves as the ideal depiction of exactly what a pandemic entail and how it affects people's health worldwide.

Epidemic

Epidemic is the term given to the widespread of disease wherein pandemic is the bigger version of what an epidemic is. The global spread of epidemic is called Pandemic while the restricted spread of same in a specific geographical area has been termed as epidemic.[3] Examples of epidemics include smallpox, measles, polio, etc.

Endemic

The consistent and constant prevalence of a disease in a community/ society/area is called an Endemic. For instance, malaria is regarded as endemic in several nations and regions.

The WHO draws its definitions of pandemics, epidemics, and endemic diseases on the rate at which a disease spreads. As a result, the distinction between an epidemic and a pandemic is not one of the disease's ferocity but rather of its frequency of transmission.

Coronavirus

Before it broke out in Wuhan, China, in Dec. 2019, no one knew about this new virus. The WHO called it a public health emergent situation after it spread around the world. On January 30, 2020, it was called a world concern[4]. "Coronaviruses are a group of viruses belonging to the family of Coronaviridae, which infect both animals and humans. Human coronaviruses can cause mild disease similar to a common cold, while others cause more severe disease (such as MERS - Middle East Respiratory Syndrome and SARS – severe acute respiratory syndrome)"[5]

1.2 Overview

Even though the law was a key part of setting up many public health standards, they haven't been fully or properly implemented, that's why India's healthcare facilities aren't as good as they could be. Although at all the levels of govt., from the central to the municipal, are involved in promoting public health through different policies and legislations. Rudolph Virchow, a nineteenth-century German physician, said that *"Medicine is a social science, and politics is nothing but medicine on a large scale.*" A physician's attention must be focused on the social ramifications and the overall function of legislation in today's rapidly changing environment. Public health objectives may be achieved via the development of a legal framework. Health law's scope has grown to suit the requirements of society just as much as the field of public health itself. When the "Universal Declaration on Human Rights (UDHR)" of 1948 was published, it outlined that *"states must provide a minimum level of conditions to ensure that everyone can benefit from the right to health and receive primary health care in an equitable manner, even though the right to health is a civil right protected by the United Nations (UN) Charter."* It is necessary to distinguish between a basic human right as well as a more particular legal & constitutional right to healthcare, such as public health laws.

Therefore, Public health legislation is nothing but rules, regulations, legislative imperatives, laws and statutes drafted with the amalgamation of the subjects of law, medicine, healthcare, and public at large in mind. The said legislations are an initiative to maintain public health and hygiene standards in society which comes within the directives of state making it a welfare state. Thus, the implementation of public health law (rules and regulations), by government and administrative bodies, is a critical component in maintaining population-level health. It lays out the legal framework for practitioners and professionals, as well as the scope of their work.

Legislations as well as policies are crucial tools for states to use in order to protect citizens from potential health threats, prevent disease, and work toward the goal of creating healthy communities. Legal agreement with the standards that belong to the same must be demonstrated on both the national & the global levels due to the presence of worldwide legislation. This legislation can take the form of global health rules or public health treaties, hence required to be studied. This research investigates their individual and collaborative roles in identifying the health and hygiene problems prevailing in the society as well as legal imperatives to solve the same.

1.3 Historical Background

1.3.1 Beginning of Public Health Law in British Regime

A significant foundation for the establishment of new healthcare systems is provided by the emergence of public health in British India in the late nineteenth and early twentieth centuries, as well as a shift from polling to microscopic medical research. The proliferation of contagious diseases and the evolution of tropical medicine were fostered by the establishment of colonial rule. History of illness and precaution in the colonial setting can be traced back to the ecology of contagious diseases, majority of ongoing traces of which can still be found in the developing countries and third-world countries to this day.

Western medicines have been used in India since 1600, when the first ship of surgeons from the British East India Company arrived. The Company achieved its authority over India in the year 1757, which resulted in the formation of municipal & military services throughout the nation. As part of the Company's efforts to provide medical care for its troops and employees in Bengal, a medical group was established in 1764. Overall, 28 surgeons mainly composed the team during that time, including four head surgeons and eight assistants. Later, the Hospital Boards was formed in 1775. It was presided over by the Surgeon General and Physician General, both of whom worked for the "Commander-in-Chief" of the "Royal Indian Army." Medical departments with 234 surgeons were first established under British authority in province of Madras, Bengal and Bombay in 1785. The medical departments had representatives from both the military and the civilian medical departments. In the year 1796, boards were rechristened as medical boards. They were granted the authority to monitor the civil operations of medical department. The "Indian Rebellion of 1857" culminated in the transfer of governance of India to the British Crown, as well as the establishment of numerous departments of civil services. Bengal did not have a separate civil medical department until 1868, when the British established one. On January 1, 1869, two officials were appointed to the positions of Statistical Officer & Public Health Commissioner. The three medical divisions that were a part of the presidential government combined when it was abolished in 1896 to become what is today known as the Indian Medical Services.[6]

The "Army Medical Department," which later had become the "Royal Army Medical Corps," took care of the Royal Indian Army's healthcare. The central govt. had control over medical depts. up until 1919. It was decided to devolve public health, sanitation, as well as clinical information to the states after the "Montgomery-Chelmsford Constitutional Reforms (1919)".[7]

This was the initial step in India's strategy to make a centralised system for managing healthcare. In 1920 and 1921, the "Municipality and Local Board Acts" and laws to enhance individuals' health in the regions were passed. The Government of India Act, 1935 granted regional administrations greater pathway to follow. All actions that were associated with health were classified in three groups: "federal", "federal-cum-provincial" and "provincial".

In 1937, the Public Health Commissioner was made the secretary of the "Central Advisory Board of Health". This committee was in charge of devising a comprehensive strategy for public health operations across the country. "Madras Public Health Act" was passed in 1939 and was the first law ever passed in India. In 1946, the GoI constituted the "Health Assess and Development Committee" [8] to look at the nation's healthcare system and make suggestions for improvement. In 1946, the Committee gave its fact sheet, which examined the nation in terms of public health, "Medical Relief", "Professional Education", "Medical Research", and "International Health".[9] One of the Indian Medical Service most important positions was that of civil medical official or executive director. Director General had to follow the medical board's instructions because he was the head of the medical department. The GoI had a person in charge of hygiene, vaccination, and keeping track of people's births and deaths. The Health Commissioner as well as the Statistical Officer were in charge of the public health. The responsibility for collecting polls, planning, coordinating, programming, as well as controlling all health problems in the nation was given to the central staff. The govts. of each province were responsible for overseeing their separate provincial medical depts. Key advisors to the govt. included the Sanitary Commissioner for the region, the "Inspector General of Civil Hospitals" (also called "the Surgeon General in Madras & Bombay"), as well as the Director. Deputy Surgeon Generals and Assistant Inspectors provided assistance to the Surgeon Generals and "Inspector General of Civil Hospitals" respectively. Authorities at the provincial level were responsible for planning, managing, and monitoring all healthcare facilities. A medical officer who was recognized as the Civil Surgeon was in charge of supervising the arrangements made for the district's sanitary and medical needs. The job duties included supervising all facets of people's health as well as keeping an eye on healthcare facilities. At least three times a year, higher government officials were required to examine rural hospitals and clinics, perform medico-legal obligations, and engage experts. They were identified as having responsibility for tasks connected to sanitation and public health, such as giving vaccinations and maintaining sensitive data. In Madras, the position of Civil Surgeon was referred to as the District Medical & Sanitary Officer. On the other hand, in Bombay, he was the only person responsible for managing the district headquarters. The duty for rural clinics & hospitals were directly under the authority of the "Surgeon General of Bombay". The "Deputy Sanitary Commissioners", of Bombay, supervised the sanitary activities & other health responsibilities for public that was governed by the civil surgeon in the several provinces. This was done under the direction of the sanitary commissioner of Bombay.[10]

Military doctors from Europe comprised the majority of the personnel in the Indian medical services, which was established in England. In 1788, Lord Cornwallis, who was India's Governor General at the time, issued rules prohibiting clinical personnel from working in civil offices unless they had served a minimum of two years in the military. This policy stayed largely in place for the rest of the century.

Calcutta Medical College opened its doors in 1835, making Indian Medical Service available to local Indians who had studied in the city and wished to work as "Assistant Civil Surgeon" in civil divisional hospitals or in the "Subordinate Military Medical Services". So, in order to prepare specialists to work as Sub-Assistant civil surgeon in rural hospitals and health centers, state medical institutions were established in the largest provincial capitals. These experts were trained at big provincial offices. In 1880, there were approximately 1200 public clinics & hospitals that were overseen by the Imperial GoI, but by 1902, that number had increased to almost 2500. In 1902, for every 330 square miles, there was one hospital. In 1880, the income of public health institutions was 3.6 million rupees, and in 1902, it was around 8.1 million rupees. In 1880, there were 7.4 million patients; by 1902, that figure had risen to almost 22 million.

1.3.2 History of vaccination in British India

Vaccines in India have been traced back to 1802, when small pox vaccine was discovered and a Superintendent General of Vaccination was established. Bombay presidency was established in 1827 with the appointment of four European superintendents and one Indian vaccinator to the position. Vaccination activities were intensified under the supervision of vaccination superintendents, who oversaw the entire process. In 1870, the Sanitary Commission & all their staff were entrusted with the responsibility of carrying out the said programme. Additional district public vaccination workers were also monitored by Civil Surgeons in addition to Deputy Sanitary Commissioner in Bombay.

In 1880, a law was passed requiring all children in towns and cantonments to be inoculated against Diseases. In those days, the primary focus was on small pox vaccination, while vaccinations against plague and other Diseases were also delivered. Initially, Variolation (an Eastern inoculation approach) was used to manage, but it was eventually dropped. Five hundred sixty-six persons were immunized in Bengal, and Punjab during the years 1864 and 1865, whereas more than five million people were immunized in the same regions between the years 1902 and 1903. In 1880 and 1881, the vaccination rate in British India was 2.7%; by 1902 and 1903, it had climbed to 3.5%, according to the World Health Organization. 19.9% of new born were successfully vaccinated at birth in 1880 and 1881, compared to 39.1% in 1902 and 1903, respectively. In 1880 and 1881, the budget for immunization was around 0.7 million rupees. In 1902, the price had grown to about 1.1 million rupees. The Act for the Registration of Births and Deaths was passed in 1873. The vital statistics department, which included the registration of deaths and births, was under the supervision of vaccination and sanitary professionals. In this era, the Indian Factories Act was passed for the very first time, and in 1881, the first ever census of the entire Indian subcontinent was carried out in order to battle various epidemics. Based on same, special official groups and commissions were established.

1.3.3 History of Disease Control and Prevention during British India

Upon gaining control of India, the British Empire was challenged with various diseases that were native to the region at that time. India was a big country with many different types of environments, including the world's highest mountains, flat green plains, dense forests, as well as dry deserts. The prevalence of diseases in the nation, which were caused by carelessness and poor preservation of natural resources as well as Indian customs and habitats, astounded the British. Due to the restricted capabilities of the Indian Medical Service, such a diverse region had its own unique ailments that were difficult to prevent. Massive amount of labor was used to be put into epidemic prevention in order to save the lives of everyone in Imperial troops. Plague, leprosy, cholera, and malaria were all epidemic illnesses that had terrible consequences throughout that time period. The British government's primary goal was to alleviate suffering and provide effective interventions because at the time, healthcare was a state obligation and there were very few private groups or volunteers. This resulted in a dearth of medical personnel and resources. Environmental hygiene and Prevention had been ignored for a long time. That it was possible to prevent many deaths didn't occur until the late 1800s, when the government realized the importance of public health services and increased their funding.

1.3.4 Public Health Law Developments in British India during Plague, Cholera and Malaria- season of epidemic continued

Plague

There have been numerous plague epidemics in India, but the most prominent was in Kutch in 1812. Before it was eradicated, it not only spread to Sind and Gujarat but also remained there for about ten years. Hansi, a town in the Hissar district of Punjab, received reports of plague-like symptoms earlier in 1828 and 1929. The Rajputana state of Marwar was said to have a significant plague occurrence in 1836. A bubonic plague outbreak erupted in Bombay in 1896, prompting the establishment of the first official records in the city. It was first detected in Bombay, Pune, Calcutta, and Karachi, all of which are port towns. Except for a few isolated cases in other regions of the country during the first year, it was restricted to Bombay. In the 2nd year, outbreaks were discovered in Mysore, Madras, Bengal, the United Provinces, Punjab, the Central Provinces, Kashmir, as well as Hyderabad.[11] It ravaged practically the whole country of India till around 1899. As per official numbers, about 2 million people died from the deadly disease by the end of 1903. However, the true figure could be much higher. India was on the world trade route because of this reason, the British Imperial administration of India was under enormous pressure to contain the emergency. The Plague Commission was created in 1896 by Professor T.R. Frasor, a professor of "Materia Medica" at the University of Edinburgh. People from a variety of backgrounds participated on the committee, notably Indian Interior Secretary J.P. Hewett as well as Army Medical School Netley Prof. A.E. Wright. The Plague Commission stated in their report, which was published in 1904 that the disease was extremely contagious and humans were a significant source of disease spread since through them pathogens are transported. Restricting mass transportation and improving sanitation facilities were recommended as crucial preventative measures by the commission. Additionally, the health services of public were required to be improved and labs should be built, according the report stated.[12] As a result, the India's Epidemic Diseases Act, 1897 came to picture. The act demonstrated a variety of ideas, including the use of colonial power to ruthlessly separate sick people, clean them, relocate them, and even demolish diseased buildings. Anyone on a train or ship might be detained by medical and administrative personnel if they were deemed suspect. This made the native people very worried, and there were even riots in some places. However, the govt. used armed forces to make sure that the necessary precautions were taken correctly. Extensive research was conducted.[13] It was decided to create the Plague Research Committee. Surgeon Maj. Lyons, President of the Plague Investigation

Committee including Surgeon Capt.[14] Hankin. (Whose research showed that plague bacillus was not distributed saprophytically from the outside surroundings but as a result of poor hygiene, animal, and human excrement spread rapidly.) W.B. Bannerman, who was in charge of the "Bombay Plague Research Laboratory" from 1897 to 1900, in one of his reports concluded that the anti-plague vaccine developed by Dr. Waldemar Haffkine were carried out on a massive scale successfully. To supervise the preventative efforts, five plague committees were formed. M.E. Couchman's Reports on "Bubonic Plague Administration" in Bombay (1896–1897);[15] "Brig. Gen. W.F. Gatacre", Chairman "Plague Committee for the year 1896–97";[16] "Sir James MacNabb Campbell", Chairman "Plague Committee for the year 1897–98";[17] the "Municipal Commissioner of Bombay" for the years 1898 to 1901;[18] as well as "Capt. J.K. Condon" for the years 1896–1899 "Maj. E. Wilkinson", "Chief Plague Medical Officer", as indicated by his studies on plague treatment as well as vaccination in plague-infected districts of Punjab & its dependents (1901–1903).[19]

Cholera

Prior to 1817, cholera had only been observed in Bengal; however, the cholera epidemics that swept across India from 1817 to 1821. It was a major shock for the British East India Company. By the 1830s, the western world had recognized cholera as a potentially fatal disease and further its devastating impact on the Company's troops and commanders, it became the focus of medical services in India; otherwise, it was considered a poor people's sickness. There was no effective therapy for cholera at the time, the emphasis was on prevention. Following the Constantinople International Sanitary Conference in 1868, the British Indian administration clung to metrological views concerning cholera, thinking that atmospheric conditions were the primary cause of disease propagation. The Committee of Cholera was founded in 1868 as a response to the cholera epidemic that occurred in India the previous year. Their objective was to research the causes & origins of the disease. Researchers investigated the factors that lead to the growth of cholera, the prevalence of the disease in India (both as an epidemic and also as an endemic), the disease's tendency to be transmitted to others and spread, as well as the preventative measures that are required. Following the investigation, they came to the conclusion that cholera was widespread, particularly during religious festivals and fairs. The epidemic was brought on by a virus that was carried by soldiers, pilgrims, and travelers. The group proposed that institutions such as hospitals, jails, and military cantonments improve their hygiene, provide good festival management, and establish sanitary conditions in their respective facilities. "Dr. S.C. Townsend", the Sanitary Commissioners for the "Central Provinces and Berar", also wrote about his research into a cholera outbreak that occurred in 1868.[20]

In the 1860s and 1870s, epidemiologist Dr. James L. Bryden, India's first and government's leading expert on epidemic cholera, undertook extensive research on the cholera pandemic. While serving in Bengal as a "statistics officer" for the "Indian Medical Service", he witnessed cholera in action. He in his research suspected that cholera was an airborne infection spread by a creature that looked like a seed and the virus is not disseminated by polluted drinking water. Moreover, Punjab's sanitary commissioner, A.C. DeRenzy, objected the idea on the grounds that it would compromise India's attempts to stop the transmission of cholera in the area. Even John Murray, the North Western Bengal Civil Hospitals Inspector General, has spent a lot of time researching cholera. According to him, environmental factors were responsible for cholera epidemics and may be communicable. This in fact helped in providing vital cholera treatment instructions at a time when the epidemic was occurring. Other important projects involve reports by H.W. Bellew, Deputy Surgeon General as well as sanitary commissioner for Punjab, on cholera epidemics in India from 1862 to 1881, & findings by Commissioner Benarus Division on disease epidemics in the Bulliah sub-division & Mirzapore area (United Provinces). W.R. Cornish intended those metrological theories regarding cholera be abandoned in the 1890s. New treatment options and better preventative measures arose, resulting in a significant drop in cholera mortality.[21]

Malaria

Beginning in the late nineteenth century, the situation continued to deteriorate. One of the most important aspects of the issue was the development of railroads and agricultural systems by the British administration of India without taking into account the need for suitable drainage channels for flooding as well as rainwaters. As a result, there was an abundance of fresh water reservoirs available for mosquito reproduction giving birth to malaria. Giving rise to high death rate which resulted into economic losses. In those days when the British officers, who were operating in sensitive areas such as Punjab found themselves vulnerable to the threat of malarial infection and lethal consequences. Thereafter, proper drainage became a top priority, and chemoprophylaxis with Quinine became a standard practice.

In 1882, an investigation was conducted on malaria. In August 1897, an illustration was put forth that depicted malarial parasite's life cycle, saying that anopheles mosquitoes carried protozoan parasites known as "plasmodia"[22] that caused malaria[23]. In light of this discovery, the scope of malarial parasite research was expanded, and malaria control methods were refocused on mosquito eradication as the primary means of preventing malaria. Around the year 1900, the scientists Christophers, Stephens, as well as James carried out extensive research on mosquitoes at the cantonments of military in the Indian state of Punjab. Christophers was in charge of organising both the "All-India Malaria Conferences (1900–1909)" as well as "the Punjab Malaria Surveys (1909–1911)".

The causes and control of malarial fevers were the focus of Capt. S.P. James's research from 1903 to 1908. He published extensively read papers on the prevention and treatment of malaria for medical professionals. In 1909, in Kasauli, Tanzania, a group called the "Central Malaria Bureau" was set up. Its task was to regulate & study malaria. In 1911, Captain S.R. Christophers & Dr. C.A. Bentley went to Duars to look into malaria & blackwater fever. They asserted that the tract was a hyper-endemic region for malaria, with an endemic index ranging from 50 to 100%. The prevalence of hyper-endemic malaria resulted in the creation of backwater fever. As per the WHO, large-scale tropical labour aggregation has a major effect on the epidemiology of tropical malaria. It was determined that a lack of documenting of important events, starvation, an unfair labour system, lack of sanitation, and the creation of foci involving sick immigrants all contributed to epidemics in that location. Charles A. Bentley conducted research on the causes and treatments of malaria in Bombay in 1911 in accordance with the specific directives of the Malaria Investigation Committee. His research revealed that malaria was accountable for 60–75% among all fever episodes, costing the nation as a whole 1.2 million in lost revenue. Bently advocated malaria control measures that included effective mosquito removal and drainage system improvements.[24] Deputy sanitary commissioner for "Western Registration Districts" Maj. J.L. Marjoribanks[33] conducted malaria research on the Salsette Islands as early as 1913. The results he came up with are exactly the same as those we have now. In Punjab, malaria was a major health concern. Following Christopher's initial work, the Punjab Malaria[25] Bureau carried out extensive malaria monitoring and research as a result of his findings. There was a serious outbreak of malaria in Punjab in 1918, as demonstrated by the thorough studies and descriptions of the province's "Chief Malaria Medical Officers" from 1913 to 1918, including "Capt. Clifford A. Gill (1913)", "Lt. Col. D.T. Lane (1914)", "Col. H. Hendley (1915-1917)", as well as "Colonel R.C. MacWatt (from 1917 to 1918)". Over the course of six years, the Research Scholars of these publications provide a comprehensive description of malaria control activities carried out in Punjab. Malaria fatality rates were 17.15 per 1000 people in 1913, 27.613 per 1000 people in 1915, 14.73 per 1000 people in 1916, and 66.56 per million people in 1918.[26] Malaria vectors, such as mosquitoes, were also investigated in this study. Major McGilchrist's Stegomyia study in 1912 & 1913, M.O.T. Iyengar's Study of "Malaria & Environs" in West Bengal, Calcutta as "Entomologist" to the "Dept. of Malaria Research" of Bengal in 1913, as well as Dr. K.S. Mhaskar's Mosquito Study in Karachi in 1913 were all important mosquito experiments that came after the task of Stephens & Christophers in 1900. It was criticised by[27] "the League of Nations" because the British Indian government used quinine as a chemoprophylaxis on a large scale. It was made accessible in high-risk regions like Punjab as well as the tropics in small packs comprising five to seven quinine grains for a quarter-anna at places like prisons as well as post offices. On the other hand, this was the practice until the discovery of chloroquine as well as the related suggestions given by the WHO about its application.

Influenza Pandemic

It is sometimes referred to as the Spanish Flu of 1918–19. This is reported to have killed between 20 and 50 million people globally and is regarded as the deadliest. This severe case of influenza was brought on by the H1N1 virus. Early in 1918, the disease was first recorded, and in the year end it had expanded to every nation in the world, with India thought to be its primary locus. The monsoon, which brings humidity, and an increase in the pathogenicity and mobility of the viral strain are thought to be the main contributors to the intensity and transmission of the disease.

Polio Epidemic

Up until the late 1990s, when the EPI was started, India had the worst polio epidemic among developing nations. India experienced extremely high rates of polio in both urban and rural states, with Uttar Pradesh being the worst-affected. Post-polio paralysis, which was said to be its worst aftereffect, affected roughly 6 out of every 1000 preschoolers in the Vellore district.

The oral polio vaccine was first introduced in 1964 in Bombay and then later in the year1965 in Vellore. Salk's IPV and Sabin's OPV were the options available to India. For ten years even after the OPV was added to the EPI, no difference could be observed. Nevertheless, with the government increased surveillance, the expected outcomes were obtained, and in the month of January year 2011, India was certified polio-free. Since then, focus has been placed on keeping the defense to prevent a resurrection.

Indian Journal of Public Health Research & Development, August 2019, Vol. 10, No. 8 1505 in early 1918 and later in autumn, it began to spread all around the world, India considered to be the foci [28]. The second wave of the attack began in Bombay in 1918 and spread to other parts of northern India and Sri Lanka from where it spread worldwide [29]. Improvement in the virulence and velocity of the virus strain and the monsoon bringing humidity are considered to be the key factors in increasing the severity and spread [28].

Polio Epidemic (1970-1990): India was the worst affected by polio among the developing countries until the late 1990s after which the EPI was initiated [30]. The incidence of polio in India was very high in both urban and rural states and the most affected was the state of Uttar Pradesh [31]. Its worst sequel was reported to be post-polio paralysis and in the district of Vellore, about 6/1000 preschool children were affected [32]. It was in 1964 in Bombay and 1965 in Vellore that the oral polio vaccine was introduced [33]. India had a choice between Salk's IPV and Sabin's OPV. Even after the introduction of the OPV in EPI there was no improvement to be noted for 10 years [33]. But with improvement in surveillance, the desired results were achieved and India was declared polio-free status in January 2011 and emphasis has been laid on maintaining the guard to prevent resurgence [30].

Small Pox Epidemic

In 1974, it is regarded as one of the most devastating smallpox outbreaks of the twentieth century. Around 85% of this epidemic's global impact was caused by India. This pandemic broke out in three different villages in India-West Bengal, Bihar, and Odisha but it was unable to connect the infected people, therefore it was classified as three independent epidemics. While nearly 15,000 people died in this outbreak, many others survived, but the majority of them suffered from deformities like blindness, etc. The WHO's smallpox eradication campaign succeeded in eradicating the disease. This was the first disease to be fought on a worldwide platform, and the WHO declared it exterminated in 1980.

SARS Epidemic

SARS (severe acute respiratory syndrome) is regarded as the first significant breakout of a contagious diseases in the twenty-first century. It began in the Chinese province of Guangdong in 2003 and rapidly migrated to around 30 nations in Asia, the Americas, and Europe. Within seven to eight months, it was responsible for a total of 8,439 cases and 812 fatalities.

Meningococcal Meningitis Epidemic

In India, occurrences of this epidermic suddenly increased in the early months of 2005. There have been cases reported in Delhi and the neighboring states of Uttar Pradesh and Maharashtra. As of June 2005, there had been approximately 430 cases documented. To stop the spread of disease, intervention and early detection through surveillance were used.

Chikungunya Outbreak

In Ahmedabad in the year 2006, over 3.4 million episodes of Chikungunya were detected, with a projected 2,944 deaths. As compared to the preceding four years, the fatality rate in the 2006 outbreak was significantly higher. The herd immunity to the then-isolated genotype was related to the dynamic nature of this pandemic. Major attempts were made to reduce mosquitos, and various awareness programmes were launched by both print and broadcast media.

H1N1 Flu Pandemic

The H1N1 flu pandemic commenced in May 2009 and had expanded worldwide by July 2009. By August 2010, it had been designated a pandemic, with over 18,500 deaths reported worldwide. There were three strains of influenza viruses circulating at the time, with the Inf A (H1N1) and Inf A (H3N2) viruses being substantially supplanted by the pdm H1N1 strain.

Indian Swine Flu Outbreak

It alludes to the ongoing 2009 H1N1 epidemic in India, which was still going strong as from March 2015. This 2015 episode is considered a recurrence of the virus, with the most likely causes being low temperatures, declining host immunity, and a failure of vaccination campaigns after 2010. According to NCDC data, the hardest afflicted states in India during this pandemic were Rajasthan, Maharashtra, and Gujarat.

Nipah Outbreak

The virus was discovered for the first time in Malaysia and Singapore in the late 1990s. The fruit bat is the natural host for this disease, and transmission occurs through direct person-to-person contact. The Nipah virus outbreak began in Kozhikode District, Kerala, in May 2018. This is the first Nipah virus outbreak documented in Kerala and the third in India, with the most recent previous outbreak being in 2007. The spread of information about this infection, isolation of the patients, and post-outbreak surveillance all contributed to the outbreak's containment.

Several plagues and pandemics have tested India's resilience. Good medical treatment and efficient research have enabled us to fight every sickness and, thankfully, even eradicate a few. It can be proved that many infectious diseases have spread through time because of a lack of sanitary conditions and a congested environment. The tropical environment and seasonal rains in India are yet another major component that has contributed to various infection epidemics in the past and will continue to do so in the future. Though it has been difficult to gather all of the epidemics and pandemics due to a lack of sufficient data and faults in data retention, earnest efforts have been made to include the majority of the significant ones.

1.4 Public Health – A Corollary of Right to Life under Constitution of India

The right to health isn't specifically guaranteed by the constitution of India, which means that it is not protected by Indian law. However, the Constitution contains numerous references to public health and the role of the state to provide healthcare for people. The Right is based on part IV of the Indian Constitution, which outlines the fundamental foundations of governmental policy for example - Art. 39 (E) directing the State to protect employees' health, yet Art. 42 mandates equal pay for equal effort, whereas Art. 47 requires that the State promote better health by boosting citizen's nutritional & dietary standards. Art. 243G, Municipalities as well as Panchayats have powers in addition to the States (read with 11th Schedule, Entry 23). According to the interpretation of various landmark judgments, Article 21, which provides the right to life, also ensures the right to health and healthcare. In September 2019, the 15th Finance Commission also recommended establishing healthcare a fundamental right and transferring it from the State to the Concurrent list. In the context of Indian cooperative federalism, *"public health and sanitation; hospitals and dispensaries"* is listed in the VII Schedule, state authorities are required by the constitution to develop, administer, and enforce public health regulations. States in India had unequal public health systems, based on an NITI Aayog 2019 evaluation; this difference was primarily due to a lack of technical expertise and financial constraints. It is true that state monetary dependence on the national govt which continues to be a major problem, but adding health care to the Concurrent List will result in more paperwork, institutional constraints, and bureaucracy. Even if the federal executive's political ideology would continue to influence the policy decisions of states, this centralization would strip states of their constitutional rights. An all-encompassing plan would also fail to provide each state in India the individualized attention they need. Cooperative federalism is a vital part of the Indian Constitution, but it must not be impeded by central-state collaboration on a critical issue like health.

1.5 Rationale of Study

The rationale behind the present study is research scholar's keen interest in studying qualitatively how laws have evolved from the time of British India till present modern 21st century India wherein no one ever expected that world will be in a state of pandemic and we all shall be suffering with survival issues. The scholar wishes to identified the nature of changes and challenges being followed in the legal System which has finally compelled the government to device new policies and call for reformation into the existing Public Health Laws to provide a better administrative procedure. Further, scholar in the thesis proposes to study the reforms and policies devised by government during the present Pandemic and how such policies have secured future generations if such a situation arises in future. The study here has specifically been focused on Public Health Laws merging the fields of Health, Medicine and Law to analyze the structure in accordance with the needs of society.

1.6 Hypothesis

1. The Indian public health legislation contains a variety of legislation regulations, rules, administrative decisions, and announcements dealing with many aspects of public health dimensions, and they are sufficient to provide an agreeable solution to the COVID outbreaks scenario.
2. The quarantine rule established under the 160-year-old Indian Penal Code of 1860 and the 123-year-old Epidemic Diseases Act of 1897 proved efficient in managing the dreadful COVID-19 outbreak.
3. The nationwide lockdowns imposed under Sec.6, 10, 38, & 72 of the "Disaster Management Act of 2005" aided much in coping with the tremendous issues of COVID-19.
4. When COVID-19 occurred, the "Public Health (Prevention, Control, and Management of Epidemics, Bio-Terrorism, and Disasters) Bill" (written in 2017) would have been the exact legislation to come into force.

1.7 Research Objective

1. To examine the existence of effective operating procedures that invoke relevant provisions of the identified laws including Acts, Rules, Regulations and Orders.

2. To identify key gaps in the existing system.

3. To find and define the next steps for the way forward.

1.8 LITERATURE REVIEW

Terry Carney, Bennett, and Belinda. ***"Asian Pandemic Preparedness: A Role for Law and Ethics?"*** **Asia Pacific Journal of Public Health, vol. 23, no. 3, Sage Publications, Inc., 2011, pp. 419–30.**

The Pandemic Planning law has been criticized in present study on the Asian continent, and it has been mentioned how the governments of various Asian nations cope with the severity of a pandemic utilizing their current legal texts. Again, the primary focus of this is the economic impact of a pandemic, as well as the prospect of improved implication of legal public health policies on the government as a whole.

Matthew M. Kavanagh & Renu Singh – ***"Democracy, ability, and coercion in pandemic response: COVID-19 in comparative political perspective,"*** **Journal of Health Politics, Policy and Law 45.6 (2020).**

COVID-19 has wreaked havoc in governments all over the world. Established ideas and empirical understanding were also called into question in comparative politics and health policy. There are three important things to think about: First of all, the most likely candidates, the ones who could have done the most to prevent the pandemic, did not do enough to stop it. In the perspective of COVID-19 & pandemic preparedness, how should ability be described and how can political ability be incorporated? Second, multiple studies proving the health benefits of democracy have failed to adequately explain the government's behaviour throughout this pandemic. Is it helpful to respond to disease in a dictatorial manner? Third, after decades of aggressive public health practises, COVID-19 has earned broad support for police-enforced lockdowns, isolation, and quarantine. Is it possible that these techniques will be long-term beneficial for healthly public ideas in a positive way? Even though the pandemic is still going on, this paper discusses some of these problems in new ways where decisions are too soon to make.

Binoy Kampmark. *"The Pandemic Surveillance State: COVID-19's Enduring Legacy."* Journal of Global Faultline, Pluto Journals, vol. 7, no. 1, 2020, pp. 59–70.

This paper primarily investigates and discusses the ongoing technological surveillance that the government of India has implemented, how such surveillance essentially invites dangers into the lives of citizens, and whether such technological surveillance has aided India in forming a better Public Health service or not. It also sheds light on recent changes in India's Public Health legal requirements.

Zubair Ahmed, Mohammad Rauf, and M.Z.M. Noman- *"Indian Quarantine Law Enforcement & Corona Virus (COVID-19) Pandemic"*

During the Pandemic, most Indian states and state governments grappled with the notion of implementing quarantine laws, and the reality is that after a certain point in time, the quarantine laws of the states deteriorated, and most states failed to keep their pandemic rules and regulations. As a result, this offers and attempts to recover the flaws in quarantine legislation, as well as how India's quarantine law has influenced the whole method of Pandemic & the transmission of COVID-19 in India. Furthermore, this piece fundamentally covers various recent case laws on the issue and dissects India's current quarantine law position. M.Z.M.Noman, Tarique Faiyaz, Mohammad Rauf, Saif A.Khan, Zubair Ahmed, & Madiha Tahreem. Journal of Xidian University, 12(4), 536-542 (2020).

Loewenson, Rene, et al. *"Reclaiming comprehensive public health."* BMJ global health 5.9 (2020)

It states that there have been significant disparities in the distribution and intensity of COVID-19, as well as the type and timing of reactions, among nations and situations over the last six months. Acute problems typically receive a significant attention & resources in a relatively short timeframe. COVID-19, on the other hand, is a long-term pandemic that exacerbates and deepens socioeconomic gaps, erodes health and democratic systems, and demands long-term intervention at all levels, local and global. Numerous countries' responses to COVID-19 exemplify long-standing contradictions between disparate public health systems and methods. One broadly defined approach views individual as right holder who should participate actively in proactive initiatives to alleviate health socioeconomic determinants while preserving human rights and communal safety. When epidemics threaten people socioeconomic and political interests and security, the second approach considers reactive technical, biomedical 'surveillance' operations combined with biosecurity measures that rapidly implement Research Scholaritarian and militarised approaches to protect populations from pathogens. Both approaches incorporate knowledge and technology in varying degrees and for varying reasons. COVID-19 has increased the conflict between these two paradigms, which have coexisted, disputed, and been utilized intermittently throughout the last two centuries. These changes will have a significant impact on the way health problems are seen and managed for the foreseeable future.

***"A Critique of the Indian Government's Response to the COVID-19 Pandemic,"* J. Ghosh. 519–530 in J. Ind. Bus. Econ (2020)**

This mostly focuses on how the Pandemic has altered the course of action of the Indian government and how the government has enacted legislation in order to battle the massive Pandemic difficulties across the country. Furthermore, this literature includes a thorough examination of the obsolete Indian disaster management rules that have not been amended in a long time, and the Indian government's response to the same has been heavily criticised in this area.

Watson, Marlene F., et al. "*COVID 19 interconnectedness: Health inequity, the climate crisis, and collective trauma.*" *Family process* 59.3 (2020)

A new spread of the COVID-19 infection in the US has highlighted the intricate web of linkages between globalisation, PH, financial stability, environmental protection, and social trauma. Immigrants who are either documented or undocumented experience significant discrepancies in access to as well as provision of healthcare, affordable homes and financial capacity. The purpose of this research is to analyse those specific problems and to provide faily therapists with a framework to understand them by looking at the 4 aspects: cultural norms, socioeconomic health determinants, social trauma, as well as family therapists' ethical & moral responsibilities. Families are often the strongest supporters of an economic as well as political system which actively promotes racism & class inequality, therefore it's vital to use ideas, beliefs, and practises which aren't simply palliative or realistic, but also psychological & policy-making. Health as well as critical thinking abilities should be developed and encouraged in order to better prepare experts to deal with challenges of improving health, economic equality, as well as environmental justice.

Plamondon, Katrina M. "*Equity at a time of pandemic.*" *Health Promotion International* (2021).

The goal of health improvement has always been to work toward the realisation of a world wherein every individual is afforded the opportunity to live their lives to the fullest. COVID-19, on the other hand, demonstrates considerable disparities in outcomes for people residing in and between the Global North & Global South who confront structural disadvantage in their countries. After months of a pandemic, institutionalised injustices persist, as indicated by the dramatically unequal distribution of hospitalisation and mortality across India's racial groupings. Increased awareness of the linkages of health, social institutions, and the economy enables us to live up to decades-old global promises to prioritise health justice. Decisions to act (or not act) immediately upon the occurrence of the COVID-19 epidemic are likely to create significant divisions between and within countries. Recognizing the pandemic's underlying global nature, this article examines how equity concerns are included into global reactions and concludes that such variables will have a significant impact on our global future. The purpose of this essay is to generate conversation regarding equity-cantered health promotion approaches in the context of a pandemic by examining equity considerations during a pandemic through the lens of global health research. It is believed that a focus on power and the relationship between politics and health is crucial for identifying and resolving equitable concerns.[28] This research work states conversation about how equity-cantered planning, decision-making, and action might benefit from huge societal disturbance in order to foster a more hopeful, equitable, and humane future.

Shamasunder, Sriram, and colleagues "*COVID-19 reveals weak health systems by design: why we must re-make global health in this historic moment.*" *Global Public Health* 15.7 (2020)

The COVID-19 pandemic highlights how critically important it is for global healthcare systems to both develop and restore damaged systems. The epidemic, in particular, shows how hollow the story of global health equity is, how weak the worldwide health initiative created by health security is, and how serious the health effects of power imbalances aren't only around the world, but also in regions and in individual communities. Such injustices are examined in this paper, and the researchers urge on govts., international agencies, academic institutions, as well as non-governmental organisations (NGOs) to collaborate at this pivotal time in history. We must all work together to reform the world's health care system and practises before the disease – which has already reached the Global South – spreads further and has potentially catastrophic repercussions.

Forman, Lisa, & Jillian Clare Kohler - "*Global health and human rights in the time of COVID-19: Response, restrictions, and legitimacy.*" *Journal of Human Rights* 19.5 (2020)

The COVID-19 virus outbreak has hurt people's rights since it has been used as an excuse for police abuse, Research Scholaritarian power grabs, and widespread corruption. With restricted healthcare in non-COVID-19 nations, affected populations at risk of infectious disease and adverse social & health effects, and prisons making poverty, domestic abuse, and mental health problems even worst, it has been extremely difficult for both high-income as well as low-income nations to check, track, and cure people properly In the event that COVID-19 impedes healthcare systems that are already under-resourced and people are compelled to bear the costs of testing & treatment, they become more susceptible to failures in the healthcare system, a rise in the number of fatalities from a multiplicity of factors, as well as rise in poverty & instability. COVID-19 emphasises the critical need for clarification of appropriate restrictions on the right to health in the event of a pandemic, as well as the importance of post-pandemic global health policy defence measures. In this research, important health issues like universal therapy and eliminating possible barriers to the creation of future COVID-19 medications and vaccinations are discussed. These issues are of critical importance. In the final half of the paper, the authors discuss the consequences of the pandemic for the promotion of right to health.

Dodds, Klaus, and colleagues "*The COVID-19 pandemic: territorial, political and governance dimensions of the crisis,*" (2020).

Natural disasters and austerity measures, such as pandemics, highlight the fact that we are not all in this together. Certain individuals have an unequal capacity to act and react, whereas others have several opportunities to profit. Despite the emphasis on European citizens and their experiences with lockdown, public health restrictions have successfully exacerbated additional disadvantages in other nations, such as India, prior to the virus's introduction. In March 2020, India declared a state of lockdown, leaving citizens and migrants unable to return, let alone leave the nation. Suicides and accidents surged as a result of the devastation caused by the loss of money and livelihood, especially among the most vulnerable, who struggled to cope with the disruption's intensity. Indian and Pakistani migrants have accused their respective Middle Eastern countries of refusing to aid them in returning home. When labour markets collapsed, embassies and missions on the ground were forced to offer emergency supplies. The economic & social regions impacted by the epidemic are a stark reminder of the precarious character of daily living for hundreds of millions of populations worldwide. Due to the fact that other newspapers publish declarations, special issues, and editorials, our work is to engage readers in the regions, policies, and government, as well as to create debates about the rapidly changing concerns that many regard as the global crisis. This publication is looking for academic researchers & commentators who are engaged in the relationship between the 3 terms from the past ten years: area, politics, as well as administration.

Raina, Sunil Kumar, and colleagues *"Are we prepared? Lessons from Covid-19 and OMAG position paper on epidemic preparedness."* Journal of Family Medicine and Primary Care 9.5 (2020)

Our failure to effectively combat diseases was once again highlighted by the COVID-19 outbreak. The majority of nations have pledged to emerge stronger from this calamity, and world leaders have shown a strong commitment to defending their citizens. Additionally,

Covid-19 taught us a few things that will benefit us in the future. One such lesson is that, in recent decades, the emphasis has shifted dramatically away from communicable viruses, culminating in the neglect of communicable diseases in the global health infrastructure. As a result, the present pandemic has served as a catalyst for change. The Organized Medicine Academic Guild (OMAG), which is a professional umbrella organisation, formed a committee of health specialists in order to develop a policy paper on epidemic readiness. The intention behind this was to reduce the severity of the damage that outbreaks like COVID-19 have.

Nomani, M. Z. M., & Parveen, R. "*COVID-19 pandemic and disaster preparedness in the context of public health laws and policies*". Bangladesh Journal of Medical Science, (2021).

The "National Disaster Management Research Scholarity (NDMA)" is critical in managing and propagating the COVID-19 pandemic via a multi-component approach consistent with the WHO's Disaster Management Cycle Directive. Because of the pandemic caused by COVID-19, India's healthcare system has shifted its emphasis of disaster management away from reducing risks and more toward responding to emergencies regarding public health. India adopted the five-point Disaster Management strategy in response to its tough and enlightening experiences with disaster management and the COVID-19 outbreak. The concept is demonstrated through a social experiment, a proactive approach, employee management, cooperation, planning, and teamwork.

Taghizade, S., Chattu, V. K., Jaafaripooyan, E., & Kevany, S. *"COVID-19 pandemic as an excellent opportunity for Global Health Diplomacy"*. Frontiers in Public Health, (2021).

COVID-19 is neither the first nor the deadliest pandemic in human history, and experts believe it is unlikely to be the last. There is little doubt that the global health systems have been confronted with a significant challenge. Because of this, many individuals are reconsidering how important it is to collaborate on a national, regional, as well as global level whenever there is a crisis. It is probable that the expansion of the coronavirus may lead to an upsurge in nationalism, economic expansion, as well as political power struggles on a global scale. International cooperation on a variety of levels will result in improved health, economic prosperity, and security as an alternative to unilateral action. International organisations may opt to act in accordance with the existing situation in the event of a future catastrophe. Global collaboration, global solidarity, and multilateralism are the only viable options for dealing with the pandemic threat today. It is possible to expand the scope of Global Health and Development and continue to implement it in order to improve five critical areas of the world: "international cooperation and solidarity"; "global economic, commercial, and development security"; "global health security"; and "enhancing the health system & resolving healthcare discrepancies". The creation of the COVID-19 vaccine in various nations is being affected by significant geopolitical changes & nationalistic feelings at this point.

Anirudh Prasad, Centre and State Powers under Indian Federalism, Deep and Deep Publications, New Delhi, 1981.

The book is about the analysis of the structure of how powers are divided, judicial interpretation of residuary powers, settling disputes between State & Union laws, how the State & Union work together, and how judges evaluate regulatory entries.

Paras Diwan, *"Indian Constitution Law"*, Allahabad Law Agency, Allahabad, 1994.

"The author states that the Indian Constitution is a creation of the people of India, the State themselves being created by the people of India. The Constitution is federal in form but it is not federation based upon agreement of the component States."

M.P Jain, *"Indian Constitution Law"*, Wadhwa & Company, Nagpur, 2003

The author performed an investigation comparing India with Canada, the U.S., & Australia in terms of how power is shared between the Centre as well as its components. He focuses on the historical developments that led to the establishment of federal governments in these nations.

Durga Das Basu, *"The Shorter Constitution of India"*. Wadhwa & Company, Nagpur, 2006.

The author throws light on the various judgements of the Apex Court in which it is held by the Court that though India is federal in character yet due to present needs and circumstance, it is not federal in strict sense.

Goel, S L, (2006), *"Encyclopaedia of disaster management - vol. 1-3"*. - Deep and Deep, New Delhi Green Paper on Disaster Management, (1998).

The 3 volumes written by Goel (2006) serve as a reference for comprehending the theory of disaster management (DM) as well as the problems that are associated with it. Volume 1 is on "disaster management policy and administration"; Volume 2 is on "management of natural disasters", and Volume 3 is on "management of man-made disasters". Each volume goes into depth about the topic as well as what the govt. can do to stop disasters.

Sanjaya Kumar Das, *"Centre-State relationship in the era of Coalition Politics"*, Madhya Pradesh Journal of Social Sciences, Vol. 15, No. 1, June 2010,

pp. 117-124.

In his article titled *"Centre-State Relationship in the Era of Coalition Politics,"* Sanjaya Kumar Das explains that the background of federalism and centre-state ties in India is marked by political movements & periodical struggle to form a more federal set-up. Although such attempts haven't yet resulted in major constitutional reforms toward a more federal direction, the struggle hasn't been entirely useless. In 1950, India adopted a parliamentary federal constitution having similar features of the Canadian Constitution which can be accredited to the British colonial heritage in both countries. India's leaders were educated in the tradition of liberal democracy than the leaders of the two great Asian States i.e. the Soviet Union and Communist China. At the same time, Jawaharlal Nehru was devoted to democratic socialism, agrarian redistribution, and a planned economy and for the success of these policies; he highly believed that there had to be centralized direction. It will be beneficial to examine the complicated trend toward federalism. From the beginning of the country's history until the 1960s, nation-building & development were the primary concerns of India's rulers. Jammu & Kashmir as well as Nagaland in the north-east had separatist concerns, and these were considered more as threats to national unity as well as security concerns. During this time, the campaign for centralization got started. This was also the time when the Congress was in charge of both the Centre and the States.

Mokbul Ali Laskar, "*Dynamics of Indian Federalism: A Comprehensive Historical Review*", Notion Press, Chennai, 2015, pp. 120-121.

Mokbul Ali Laskar in his work *"Dynamics of Indian Federalism: A Comprehensive Historical Review"* has asserted that globalization has had a mixed impact on the process of federalization in India. "The economic liberalization increases the autonomy of not only the private sector but also the state governments in the area of economic activities. One of the most important aspects of post-1991 economic reforms is the way in which the Central Government signed the Uruguay Round of Global Trade Negotiations and joined the World Trade Organisation (WTO) in 1995 and had its impact on the Centre-State federal dynamics in India. The Central GoI has a sovereign and exclusive right under Art. 253 of the IC to enter into international bi-lateral and multi-lateral agreements, treaties or conventions. But the Central government had to face various challenges from the states when it was making various trade-related negotiations under the WTO in 1990s. The Government of India without making consultations with the states have signed the multi-lateral treaty of WTO in 1994. However, when it came for practical operation of the WTO negotiations beginning with January 1995, the State governments had raised voices against various combative issues of WTO provisions already negotiated."

Pandey, Rajendra Kumar. *"Legal Framework of Disaster Management in India."* Indian Law Institute Review (2016): 178-190.

The Indian Constitution doesn't include any provisions that are specifically related to the disaster management. In spite of the fact that it is one of the oldest constitutions in the world, the absence of provisions for disaster management in the Constitution of India is mainly due to 3 different factors that are all connected to one another. In this research paper, Scholar also says that the DM hasn't become a way for the center and the states to compete with each other. This is because the activities associated with disaster management are meant to help people and make the world a better place. However, the matter will continue to be a possible point of controversy between the center & the states in the future."

Sarkar, Subhradipta, and Archana Sarma. "Disaster Management Act, 2005: A Disaster in Waiting?" ***Economic and Political Weekly*** **(2006): 3760-3763.**

The "Disaster Management Act (DMA)", which was approved in 2005, includes provisions for the formulation, implementation, and execution of DM plans at all levels of govt., beginning with the central govt. and moving down to the district and municipal levels. Furthermore, it ignores crucial factors, like the categorization of disasters, the identification of disaster-prone zones, the streamlining of tasks, and the participation of local populations."

Djalante, Riyanti, Rajib Shaw, and Andrew DeWit. "*Building resilience against biological hazards and pandemics: COVID-19 and its implications for the Sendai Framework.*" Progress in Disaster Science (2020).

COVID-19 will need to be addressed in 2020 according to the scholars in this article. 2020 year was projected to be a "super year" for sustainable management, advocating the necessary reforms to attain the 2030 target. The phrase "super year" comes from the phrase "super year" for sustainable development. The researcher concluded that one or both of these things can and should take place in 2020. As a result, they believe that an increased usage of the "health-emergency disaster risk management (Health-EDRM)" framework is necessary to strengthen the measures that are now being implemented to COVID-19 and the possible danger of similar occurrences in the future. In order to prove their point, they analyzed the existing responses to COVID-19 as well as the consequences these responses have for the SFDRR. We believe current disaster prevention systems and approaches, as mentioned in SFDRR, can boost responses to infections or global pandemics such as COVID-19. In this framework, we generate a variety of proposals that are both generic & unique to DRR. Providing science and information to better comprehend health and disaster-related emergencies, as well as expanding "disaster risk governance (DRG)," are some of these recommendations.

Panchenko, OlhaIvanivna. ***"The role of police in overcoming the pandemic."*** **Amazonia Investiga 9.28 (2020): 3-5**

If the incidence & development of particular conditions may be forecasted or anticipated, typical ad hoc procedures must be devised to prepare police personnel and operational assistance. It's important to know what resources are available, how the detachment is structured, and how it will respond to different emergency scenarios. These plans should also identify who will be responsible for executing the plan, as well as the specifics of their roles and responsibilities, and also the action plans for numerous emergency scenarios."

Patel, Bimal N. "*National Security of India and International Law.*" National Security of India and International Law. Brill Nijhoff, 2020.

The work looks at both old and new problems and issues, such as water, natural resources, how to deal with refugees, the use of force, nuclear principle, advancements in space, defence procurement & industrial production, as well as private organisations. This new field of research will be open to exploration, teaching, and discussion.

Nair, A. "*Covid opportunity for India.*" (2020): 15-15.

After the sudden declaration of lockdown, lakhs of migrant workers from more industrialised & urbanised cities & states moved back to villages in states with mostly rural areas and few resources. This was one of the most disturbing & overwhelming things to see. There is sufficient evidence from the course of history to show that a crisis of such scale has the capacity to revolutionize the way in which the world, nation, and society is organised and functions.

Singh, Manish Kumar, and YadawanandaNeog. "*Contagion effect of COVID 19 outbreak: Another recipe for disaster on Indian economy.*" Journal of Public Affairs (2020): e2171.

This article manages to look at COVID-19 in India from an economic point of view by using some statistics and economic data. The information obtained for the macro economy, the transportation sector, travel & tourism, human resources, the stock market, and commerce are used as the basis for the research. If the administration is unable to implement a comprehensive legislative framework, India may soon experience a health crisis and a severe economic recession."

Lee, Tsung-Ling. "*Legal preparedness as part of COVID-19 response: the first 100 days in Taiwan.*" BMJ Global Health 5.5 (2020): e002608

Economic & social concerns posed by COVID-19 would necessitate worldwide cooperation. The national response team doesn't currently include ethicists or social scientists; yet, there is a critical need to institutionalise a moral system for managing healthcare during emergencies and preventing the psychological & physical exhaustion of health practitioners. In spite of the fact that most people comply with the health precautions, the COVID-19 quarantine has an additional difficulty because it is hampered by those who are somewhat non-compliant.

Rai, Balram, Anandi Shukla, and Laxmi Kant Dwivedi. "*COVID-19 in India: predictions, reproduction number and public health preparedness.*" MedRxiv (2020).

Because of its widespread spread, COVID-19 has become a global public health emergency, according to the researcher who delivered the keynote address. In the recent past, there was an upsurge in the total number of cases that have been reported in India. Statements made for the COVID-19 can give a general idea of how the disease spreads, which helps policymakers figure out how well the healthcare system works.

Currie, Geoff. *"A Lens on the Post-COVID19 "New Normal" for Imaging Departments."* Journal of Medical Imaging and Radiation Sciences (2020).

Even though there have been a lot of initiatives during the COVID-19 emergency, it is important to think about which of these (and what other) approaches could be used after COVID-19 gets better. There should be a set of rules or practises that all imaging depts. follow.

1.9 Methodology

The present study confined to the use of doctrinal research methodology the researcher, has consulted a wide range of materials, including papers from eminent jurists as well as experts and authors, national and international judgements along with various international agreements and treaties. There are both primary and secondary data sources included in the study. It takes into consideration all applicable laws, conventions, and higher court rulings. Examples of primary materials include parliamentary debates, international conventions, and more. Journals, prominent author books, national and international research papers, journals, articles and editorials in various media, websites and other secondary sources are some examples of this type of primary source material. Analytical, evaluative, and descriptive methodologies will be used to finish my research and provide suggestions. The research is conformed to the most recent edition of the Bluebook.

Research Strategy

The research strategy followed in the present research subject is Applied or Action research strategy.

Research Method

The research method undergone is qualitative. One as while its applicability can be inferred to large number of populations though which is a key feature in quantitative method, but since the research is doctrinal and there is no survey analysis. In light of previous research and statistics that are currently available, the population has been assessed. All the analysis and observations are based on author's personal judgement and the recommendations suggested are also based on personal opinions of Author/Researcher.

Research Approach

A descriptive study research approach has been followed in the present subject to broadly describe one single subject in detail.

Data Collection Methods and Tools

For the purpose of data collection, primary data has been collected through online forums, websites, library, books and groups.

Research Process

After the collection of entire data from relevant research papers, dictionaries, books, online forums, websites, Author disintegrated the relevant extracts from collected data after duly analysing and reading them, formed a conceptualizing opinion as well as recommendations, integrated the relevant excerpts, noted down the appropriate analysis in the form of pointers and proceeded with elaborating the pointers in present subject.

Data Analysis

Author has done descriptive data analysis after collection of entire data and studying in detail to build suitable conclusion.

Ethical Considerations

There are certain ethical issues with respect to the present subject vis-à-vis utilizing scientific techniques on offenders and reliability on its evidentiary value which author has made consideration to as well as tried to remove the same by providing suitable recommendations.

Research Limitations

Following are the research limitations that have been observed by the author while approaching present subject:

Due to lack of live statistics, Author can only put forth and deal with the analysis based on author's opinions derived from pre available data.

Author has given its own purview of dealing with the ethical issues pertaining to above said subject but, author is unable to deal with vast purviews which could have been obtained in the form of different opinions and contradictions as obtained through live statistics.

1.10 Scope of the Study

The coronavirus outbreak (COVID-19) that began in 2019 has sparked a worldwide catastrophe. Even while the Indian government has made some efforts, the sheer vastness of the country has made things far more difficult for hundreds of millions of people. Medical experts have a key role in aiding the persons who are blind during this time period of their lives. The scope of this research will expand through an in-depth analysis of the current situation pertaining to the implementation of legal scenario aiming at securing the suggestive legal framework for the issues involved. This research will go into the question and look forward to find solution to it.

1.11 Significance of the Study

The corona virus is a newly identified infectious disease. Given national legislation and regulations enabling the public health approach offered by the nation's health policies, this pandemic has prepared our Indian governments in diverse and interesting levels. The present thesis is an initiative by the scholar to study each and every aspect of medico-legal developments and analyzing them to conclude the needs of society during pandemic, which has changed the entire framework of public health legal framework. The present study significantly deals with development and reforms in the area of public health laws. Hence, paving a way for future generations and making them prepared for the future epidemics. Also, the present study will suggest and propose need of certain bills, amendments and legislations to be implemented for eliminating the loop holes and lacunas present law contains.

1.12 Conclusion

Public health legislation is required to recognize the need of controlling people's changeable patterns of behavior in order to increase the community's capacity against public health threats including, in particular, cigarette use, nutrition and exercise. Such legislations may have limits, and the degree of efficacy and enforcement might have an impact on a law's ability to achieve its intended public health aims. Nonetheless, as a result, laws should not be seen as a sole means of achieving public health objectives, but rather as one among several.

1.13 Chapterisation

- **Chapter 1 – Introduction:** The goal of this chapter is to give readers a complete overview of the chapter's topic. Problem descriptions, limitations, significance and literature reviews will also be covered in this section. The study's research methodologies are also discussed.
- **Chapter 2 – A Comparative Study of Nations Handling COVID-19 Pandemic and Role of WHO:** This chapter concentrates on a comparative examination of Covid-19 countries and a discussion of the WHO's role.
- **Chapter 3 – Legal Dimension of COVID-19 in India:** This chapter focuses on the role of the 2005 Disaster Management Act, the Epidemic Diseases Act of 1897 alias Epidemic Diseases (Amendment) Act, 2020, and other relevant legislation. As part of a cooperative federalism approach, the power, structure, and operation of disaster management agencies at all levels of government will be reviewed. This chapter is critical because it is at the heart of the study. It will go over the PH Mission (Prevention, Management, Control, and Epidemics, Bio-Terrorism, and Disasters) Bill, which was drafted in 2017, and its relevance in the case of a pandemic, if relevant at the time. It will also deal with various judicial pronouncements with

respect to covid 19 and other public health legislations that have taken place till now.

- **Chapter 4 – National Lockdown-An Approach to Cooperative Federalism:** This chapter examines the effects of various state actions within the context of cooperative federalism, as well as their effects on the maintenance of peace & order.
- **Chapter 5 – Conclusion & Suggestions:** This chapter concludes with a variety of evaluations and ideas for appropriate legislation, norms, and policies, as well as various efforts and countermeasures in response to this unexpected disaster.

Footnotes

1 Webster N.- *American Dictionary of English,* MERRIAM WEBSTER, (Sept. 7, 2021, 10:28pm) https://www.merriam-webster.com/about-us/americas-first-dictionary.

2 Clemow F.- "*Pandemic of influenza*" 1, LANCET, (1894).

3 National Institute of Health- "*Understanding emerging and re-emerging infectious diseases*" National Library of Medicine (Sept. 7, 2021, 10:40 pm) https://www.ncbi.nlm.nih.gov/books/NBK20370/.

4 "WHO- "*Statement on the second meeting of the International Health Regulations 2005, Emergency Committee regarding the outbreak of novel coronavirus*", WORLD HEALTH ORGANIZATION (Sept. 7, 2021, 10:46 pm), www.who.int/news-room/detail/30-01-2020-statement-on-the-second-meeting-of-the-international-health-regulations-(2005)-emergency-committee-regarding-the-outbreak-of-novel-coronavirus-(2019-ncov)."

5 supra

6 At present referred as the Indian Health Service.

7 The reforms take their name from Edwin Montagu, the Secretary of State for India from 1917 to1922, and Lord Chelmsford, the Viceroy of India between 1916 and 1921. The

reforms were outlined in the Montagu-Chelmsford Report, prepared in 1918, and formed the basis of the Government of India Act 1919.

8 Also known called the Bhore Committee

9 Mark Harrison- Public Health in British India: Anglo Indian Preventive Medicine 1859-1914, (Cambridge University Press, 1994).

10 Government of Punjab- Punjab Medical Manual-https://highcourtchd.gov.in/sub_pages/left_menu/Rules_orders/high_court_rules/vol-III-pdf/chap18partA.pdf (Last accessed on- Sept 7, 2021).

11 Nathan R- The Plague in India 1896-1897. (Government Central Print Office 1898).

12 Lamb G-The Etiology and Epidemiology of Plague. a Summary of the Work of the Plague Commission. Issued Under the Authority of the Government of India, (2010).

13 Supplement to the Account of Plague Administration in the Bombay Presidency from September 1896 till May 1897, https://digital.nls.uk/indiapapers/browse/archive/74458388?mode=gallery_list&sn=1 (Last Accessed on Sept, 7, 2021).

14 Lyons RW, Childe LF.I. –" *Report by Surgeon-Major Lyons, I.M.S., President of the Plague Research Committee. II. - Report by Surgeon-Captain Childe, I.M.S. III. - Summary of work carried on by Mr. Hankin.*", (1897).

15 Couchman ME-. "*Account of plague administration in the Bombay Presidency from September 1896 till May 1897*", G.C.P., (1897).

16 Gatacre WF- "*Report on the bubonic plague in Bombay: 1896-97*" T.O.I, (1898).

17 Campbell JM, Mostyn R.- "*Report of the Bombay Plague Committee, appointed by government resolution no. 1204/720P, on the plague in Bombay, for the period extending from the 1st July 1897 to the 30th April 1898*" T.O.I., (1898).

18 Municipal Commissioner's Office Bombay (India)- "*Report of the Municipal Commissioner on the plague in Bombay for the year ending 31st May 1899"* T.O.I., (1898).

19 Condon JK- "*The Bombay plague: being a history of the progress of plague in the Bombay presidency from September 1896 to June 1899_compiled under the orders of government",* B.E.S., (1900).

20 G.O.C.- "*Rules regarding the measures to be adopted on the outbreak of cholera or appearance of small-pox: (G.O.C.C. No. 193 dated 3. Aug. 1870)*", S.G.P., (1870).

21 Bellew HW. –"*Cholera in India, 1862 to 1881: Bengal Province, 1862 to 1881, and review",* B.S.P., (1884).

22 Ross R.- "*Report on the cultivation of Protesoma, Labbe, in grey mosquitoes."* S.G.P., (1898).

23 In 1902, the said research was knighted and obtained the "Nobel Prize in Medicine" for his offerings and aids to medicine.

24 Bentley CA.- "*Report of an investigation into the causes of malaria in Bombay and the measures necessary for its control"* G.C.P., (1911).

25 MacWatt RC. –" *Report on malaria in the Punjab during the year 1918 together with an account of the work of the Punjab Malaria Bureau"* S.G.P.P., (1919).

26 Gill CA.- "*Report on malaria in the Punjab during the year 1913 together with an account of the work of the Punjab Malaria Bureau"*S.G.P.P., (1914).

27 Mhasker KS. –"*Report of an investigation in regard to the prevalence of stegomyia" and other mosquitoes in Karachi, and the measures necessary for their control.*" G.C.P., (1913).

28 Nomani, M. Z. M., and Faisal Sherwani. *"Security and safety of health care professionals during covid-19 pandemic in the context of epidemic diseases (amendment) ordinance, 2020.*" IJET 11.4 (2020): 23-26.

02
CHAPTER

A COMPARATIVE STUDY OF NATIONS HANDLING COVID-19 PANDEMIC AND ROLE OF WHO

2.1 Introduction

If we go even two years back to December 2019 when COVID-19 struck the entire world, starting in China and spreading on to the entire world, the term "Pandemic" was not a term of common use. This has been a big outbreak - a phenomenon that occurs once in a century. After the devastating transmission of the Spanish flu, this widespread occurrence has been able to take the number one position, bringing the nations into a scenario similar to that of a war, with people battling for their existence while simultaneously being at war with a sickness.

In the first half of the year, India was praised for its prompt response to Covid in the form of a lockdown and other stringent measures taken by the Indian government to ensure the lockdown was properly enforced. However, shortly after the lockdown was imposed, the negative repercussions of the lockdown were revealed. According to some scholars, it is not COVID-19 virus that has provided India with such a destructive result but it is the response of the government as a whole which has led to negative GDP, declining economy, increase in unemployment and lack of medical facilities. In order to maintain a strong accord to all the guidelines of WHO (World Health Organization), India led its citizens suffered into a pit of hunger, poverty, unemployment which essentially affected the method of containing virus transmission amongst people as well[1].

However, the surprising question that comes during such a discussion is that whether other countries have also faced similar adversities and destructive impact of Covid-19 situation? Whether the results of their implemented set of standard rules, regulations and protocols have been sufficient in fighting off the situation? and whether or not they had a negative impact of all the actions taken just like India in meeting the demand-supply curve of their economy? Though one can target unsuccessful government policies and a negligent administrative approach to be the factors leading to failure of controlling the situation, people being disobedient towards the said policies and trying their best to breach them as and when required was also one of the contributory factors in worsening the situation[2]. Hence, before answering the above said questions raised, it is extremely important to understand that while handling and cooperating with the COVID-19 situation, every other nation had different factors to deal with and it is pertinent to remember that the nations were not on the same pedestal during pandemic. While it is WHO that provided the whole world with a general guideline that would contain the mechanism to deal with spread of disease, not every other nation including India could follow it to its core[3].

In this chapter of thesis, research scholar shall be analyzing and understanding the situation of pandemic across the globe during COVID-19 first wave, second wave, third wave and how nations dealt with their own respective sovereign regions for cure and prevention of said disease. she has finally led to a comparative study between different countries inclusive of the Western, Asian and African Countries. To achieve the same, WHO guidelines have first been analyzed in an elaborate manner.

2.2 Right to Health and Healthcare – International Law

As per WHO Constitution (1946)[4], *"...the best achievable quality of health as a basic right of every human being."* - State governments are obligated by law to offer timely, appropriate, as well as inexpensive healthcare of good standard, and also to identify the fundamental health determinants like access to safe & potable water, hygiene, food; shelter; health-related data, education, and fair treatment of males & females; and fair opportunities to health-related resources. International human rights standards require that several international human right mechanisms, like the "Universal Periodic Review" or the "Committee on Economic, Social, and Cultural Rights", examine the responsibility that lies on the state to protect the right to health, comprising the distribution of "maximum available resources" to slowly reach this objective. The concept of having a constitutionally protected right to health has been incorporated in a variety of different national laws and constitutions around the world. An approach that is focused on the right to health mandates that health policies and initiatives give primary consideration to the requirements of the most marginalized members of society. This is a concept that has been repeated in the recently implemented *"2030 Agenda for Sustainable Development"*[5] and *"the Universal Health Coverage Initiative (UHCI)"*. Everyone should be able to experience the right to health no matter their ethnicity, age, race, or any other social standing they have. It is essential of the states to take action to improve any discriminatory policies, practices, or laws which may be in effect. This is done to make sure that non-discrimination and fairness are maintained. As part of the participation process, non-state actors, like non-governmental organizations, must be actively involved in all phases of the program's development and execution. This includes evaluations and interpretations at each stage of the process, as well as planning, implementation, monitoring, & interpretation.

"The right to the greatest achievable level of health" means that govts. have a clear system of defined responsibilities to make sure that everyone, no matter their racial identity, gender, or sexual preference, has the right to good health conditions. Recognized internationally human rights standards include the right to health, and this right is inseparable or 'indivisible' from the others listed above. This demonstrates that the implementation of the right to health depends on the realisation of other human rights, including, the rights to food, shelter, employment, education, information, as well as participation. Like other rights, the right to health includes both rights and responsibilities, as follows: *"Freedoms include the freedom to regulate one's own health and body (for example, sexual and reproductive rights) as well as the right to be free from government intrusion in one's affairs (for example, free from torture and non-consensual medical treatment and experimentation)."* In their communities and cultures, disadvantage and marginalisation are utilised to prevent some groups of individuals from attaining good health. One out of every 5 mortality globally is attributable to one of the most fatal contagious diseases. HIV/AIDS, Malaria, tuberculosis, as well as other illnesses adversely affect the poorest people around the world. Other disparities and inequalities, like those connected to age, gender, sexual orientation, and migrant status, maximise and worsen these illnesses. Additionally, lower-income populations and countries are being disproportionately affected by non-communicable diseases, which are typically regarded to be a problem affecting high-income nations. As per the WHO, it is mostly connected with lifestyle and behavioural variables, and also environmental factors, like safe housing, water, as well as sanitation. In addition, a focus on disadvantage reveals evidence of populations, such as indigenous populations, that are subjected to higher rates of illness and face significant obstacles in receiving high-quality and cost-effective care. Non-communicable ailments, like malignancy, heart disease, as well as chronic respiratory disease, have greater death and morbidity rates in such populations, regardless of the fact that collecting data systems are typically ill-equipped to record information on these populations. Some legislation and policies could target these groups in an effort to exacerbate their exclusion and make it more difficult for them to go to health care facilities such as prevention, therapy, rehabilitation and other forms of care.[6]

The Constitution guarantees the right to a healthcare system that provides equal opportunity for everyone to reach the best achievable level of health. Violations of human rights policies or a disdain for them might have serious implications. One of the most important factors in determining inadequate care is open or implied inequity in the provision of healthcare facilities both within the medical workforce and between the medical practitioners and patients. Mental disorder is often linked to a loss of dignity as well as independency, such as forced treatment or being put in an institution, as well as a lack of respect for a person's legal ability to make decisions that are in their own greatest advantage. Contrary to what most people think, psychological state still doesn't get much attention in public health, even though high rates of conflict, deprivation, as well as social exclusion are linked to inferior psychological and physical well-being for people with mental problems.

Human rights violations in healthcare are especially likely to take place to disabled people, people from indigenous groups, women infected with HIV, drug addicts, sex workers, as well as transgender & intersex persons. These involve forced or coerced treatments and procedures, such as the use of force in medical procedures and therapies. When it comes to well-being, a human rights-based framework provides a series of rules for creating and assessing healthcare policy and provision of services, as well as for finding discriminatory policies and unfair hierarchies that lead to different health outcomes for everyone and fighting against them. It is imperative that health-related projects and programs are devised with the goal of enhancing the right to health for all people, with a special focus on the poorest and most marginalised. The key concepts and requirements of a rights-based strategy are explained in more depth below. The World Health Organization (WHO) has said that human rights will be included into healthcare policies and practises at the national, regional, and international levels, with a focus on socioeconomic factors. Moreover, the WHO has been actively strengthening its position as a provider of technical, scientific, as well as political elite on the right to health, particularly by recognising: the ability & its Member States to adopt a human rights-based perspective to health; promoting the right to health through international law & development; and promoting human rights connected to health, like the right to health.

Considering the rights & interests of people at all stages of their life represents a thorough approach which is placed within the wider context of achieving human rights, non - discrimination, and fair allocation of resources. Accordingly, the WHO advocates a clear and defined approach which utilises existing gender, equality, & human rights methodologies to build more precise and strong approaches to health inequality. Given the interrelated nature of the paradigm, it provides the ability to depend on the underlying strengths and interrelationships of many methods in order to construct a coherent and successful plan to improve health and well-being for all people globally.

Not only does international law identify the right to health therapy, but it also recognizes the WHO's considerably more comprehensive concept of health. The fact that rights should be exercised in the context of a society shows that health & illness aren't just caused by biological or "natural" factors, but also by how humans communicate with each other.[7] Consequently, a rights-based strategy is completely in line with epidemiological evidence demonstrating that social factors are the fundamental drivers of disease.[8] A right to health in international law can be traced back to the 1948 "Universal Declaration of Human Rights (UDHR)," which was unanimously endorsed by the "United Nations General Assembly" as a universal standard for all people.[9] There is *"a right to a standard of living adequate for the health and well-being of himself and his family, including medical care and the right to financial security in the event of... sickness, disability, or other loss of livelihood due to circumstances beyond his control"* as stated in the UDHR. The UDHR doesn't specify the elements of a right to health. However, they extend beyond medical services in both content & scope.[10] In terms of human resources, the Cold War separated nations. In 1966, two accords on "civil and political rights and economic, social, and cultural rights" were released, thereby placing the entire Declaration.[11] In the "International Covenant on Economic, Social, and Cultural Rights (ICESCR)", the right to health was recognised for all people. ICESCR Article 12 defines a right to health and outlines the steps that states must *"realise progressively"*, *"to the maximum available resources"*, *"the highest attainable standard of health,"* that comprises *"the reduction of the stillbirth rate and infant mortality, as well as for the healthy development of the child"*, *"the improvement of all aspects of environmental and industrial hygiene"*, and *"the prevention, treatment, and control of epidemics."*

In the US, the language of continuous implementation and maximal resource availability, which signals differing standards for various nations, is difficult to reconcile with the absoluteness with which individuals generally see rights. Therefore, in practise, due process as well as other civil rights could be different in the same ways that they are different in principle. Instead of saying that discovering an right to health is pointless because of the huge differences between countries, particularly between the global south & north, the huge differences suggest that state obligations to safeguard well-being and health must be put into the context of international political economy, where international institutions and third-party states often have a disproportionate effect on the economies and policies of emerging developing countries. As is the case with all other human rights, the right to health requires "international assistance and participation" (Art. 2).[12]

The WHO's[13] reference to a "highest possible standard," a reasonableness criterion has been incorporated into the discourse on healthcare standards. The state must play a role in ensuring that everyone has equal access to health care. However, there are some things that the state can't change. Also, the greatest possible rule will evolve over time because of changes in medicine, population, disease, and the economy.[14] There are other international and regional agreements that recognize health as a human right and reflect a broad consensus on health protection concepts, in addition to the ICESCR. Right to health, as defined by international treaties, encompasses more than just healthcare; it also ensures that everyone has access to safe drinking water, sanitary conditions, and a healthy diet.[15] The interconnectedness of economic, social, cultural, civic, and political rights was widely recognised following World War II. More and more people are also in agreement that the right to health includes not only positive but also negative liberties (such as the right to be free from experimental or non-consensual medical treatment) (like the right to access medical services). International law says that states that sign multiple agreements have three kinds of responsibilities: (1) avoid direct breaches of the right to health, such as healthcare inequity; (2) protect the right from third-party intervention, such as environmental control by third parties; and (3) ensuring that everyone has access to dangerous drugs in order to fulfil their constitutional right. So, it is wrong to believe of the right to health as a package of services, although those services involve more than just medical care. A further step toward realising the right to health is to make sure that individuals and communities are given a genuine say in choices that define, determine, and have an impact on their well-being.

Involvement in promoting health has an ancient legacy in the field of public health, and this is well acknowledged. In addition, the number of studies addressing the role of structural health determinants as well as the political-economic environment is growing.[16] It is an important first step in understanding the rising body of evidence in As a first step in understanding the growing amount of research in social epidemiology that links health and social justice, It does this by showing the link between good health and the ability to build a democratic government that works.

The allocation of medical resources, proof of unequal treatment and discrepancies, and other similar things are looked at not just in terms of how they affect health, but also in terms of how they relate to legislation, policies, as well as practises which make it hard for people to have a say in making decisions and, as a result, make it hard to build a truly democratic society. Moreover, human rights violations to health & inability to protect or satisfy obligations in this area are interpreted under national & global statute not only in aspects of the arising social or economic difficulties, but also clearly in terms of the responsibility of the state, and to a lesser extent other actors. As a result, the human rights approach emphasizes that health is essentially political—that it is inextricably related to social context, ideology, and power frameworks - whilst also eliminating the decisions related to health policy from political judgment and putting them firmly within the realm of law. Establishing and preserving the right to health, like other international human rights obligations, is heavily reliant on judicial and legislative actions at the national level. And over seventy national constitutions recognise the right to health, and many more nations have passed laws in recent times that discuss different parts of the right to health. Also, a notable explanation of normative commitments has made it easier for treaty-monitoring committees to give more importance to possible infringements of the right to health in their "concluding observations," that are basically decisions on how well states are meeting their commitments under the right to health treaty. Furthermore, in some cases, compliance by quasi-judicial international bodies and state courts has become possible. Those who have dealt with the issue in domestic courts & regional agencies have mostly relied on the absolute minimum requirements which can be imposed on authorities under certain conditions. First and foremost, states have promised not to pass laws that move things backward. For example, a state that is running a programme to allocate antiretroviral drugs because of economic constraints can't let anything go wrong with antiretroviral drugs. Second, health policies & services should not be implemented to persons seeking care in a discriminatory way. Thirdly, states must take actions to limit the behaviour of 3rd parties who interfere with the right to health, like environmental pollution, in order to protect the right to health. And fourthly, Governments to adopt national plans and policies of initiatives to tackle public health risks.

2.3 COVID-19 and the World – How did the Nations Responded to Covid-19?

Since Dec. 2019, the world has observed an increase in Covid-19 instances, which has grown to the threshold of a worldwide pandemic. The disease has spread to several countries including the islands and it is reported that more than 200 countries have been affected by the same. In order to deal with pandemic, it was essential to change behavioural aspects opted by public at large. As the virus essentially transports from person to person through saliva and other forms of droplets. The Pandemic had taken on such a huge character by the middle of 2020, several nation's administrative authorities had taken various non-pharmaceutical measures or Nonpharmaceutical Interventions (NPIs), which effectively prescribed the residents of different countries in addition to community containment, to deal with the current pandemic crisis. Although there are noticeable differences between countries in terms of the strength and complexity of these nonpharmaceutical interventions, there are also noticeable differences within countries. The University of Oxford made a regulation index to keep track of the different sets of rules which various countries have put in place and how the governments of those countries have put non-pharmaceutical rules into place[17]. According to the Oxford index, the govt. reaction to COVID-19 is marked by significant complexities and variability, especially as it relates to policy efforts directed at pandemic control and closure.[18] *What is the reason for the disparate responses of national governments to COVID-19?*[19]. In addition to respond to the question, it is mentioned how institutional arrangements & governmental reactions in conformance with WHO have impacted the implementation of tri-national COVID-19 strategic responses: a mandatory plan in Sweden, a decree approach in China, and a boost tactic in Japan, among others, and these nations will be compared to India's pandemic response strategy as well.[20]

Also, before describing and understanding how different countries responded to the spread of the virus and how well their strategies lined up with WHO recommendations, it is worth noting and talk about what factors played a big role in understating the scenario of the disease outbreak in many countries and why there was such a big difference between how different countries dealt with it.[21]

2.4 Contributory Factors in Defusing COVID-19

It is not surprising that different cities and nations across the whole world handled the COVID-19 situation differently. While all nations were significantly impacted by the pandemic's devastation, some had more effective coping mechanisms than others. It is not always the governmental policies in adopting nonpharmaceutical interventions that aided in diffusing COVID-19 better but it was some other factors. In order to evaluate the WHO standards and the nation's active engagement in combating COVID-19 during the first wave of the outbreak, it is necessary to comprehend the significant elements that led to the divergence between Western and Eastern nations.

- **Population:** The curve varies greatly from country to country because of population differences. As it is a virus that spreads from one person to another through tiny droplets or through saliva, it can be easily concluded that the more the density per square kilometer, the more a country would be affected by it. However, recent research[22] on the subject of correlation shows that population of a country and the spread of virus only has a moderate connection.
- **Public Health:** A general structure including kind of infrastructure in relation to public health might be one of the important factors that dealt with the ongoing pandemic. While the population might have severe effects on a country, various nations like China escaped the trap of the first wave easily with the help of their well-built public health sector[23]. The general health and mortality rates of the general population contributed in the spread of COVID-19.
- **The Government Role:** The administrators and the govt. role in taking the right decision might be one of the leading factors that has created the disparity between countries and the abovementioned factors have only became a cherry on top. The overall command in dealing with the right legislation during the time of crisis is one of the contributing variations that needs to be considered.

2.5 The WHO Role – How WHO's Guidelines have Helped in Controlling the Pandemic Condition of Covid-19?

For more than 40 years, the role of international procedures has developed from focusing solely on specific diseases to more recently establishing the "International Health Regulations (IHR)" in 2005 and imposed a further basis of the WHO CEF in 2015.[24] It was already apparent in 2003 when WHO fought the severe SARS that the challenge of effectively coordinating response actions across borders would arise. It is evident that the currently adopted mechanisms in dealing with a large-scale outbreak are sluggish and disorganized, and they need to be improved. The outbreak brought to light the need for revisions to the IHR. After being put through its paces by the H1N1 influenza pandemic in 2009, the final draft of the IHR was put to the test once more when flaws in the global solution to the pandemic were exposed. An additional global health personnel as well as an emergency $1 billion fund have been recommended by the WHO for member countries in the event of a devastating pandemic in the future. However, these recommendations were put into effect[25] in 2014. The Ebola crisis demonstrated how all these measures essentially needed more legal and ethical frameworks and as a result of, for example, the imposition of trade and travel restrictions by some governments in response to the outbreak. The consecutive failure of WHO in taking necessary steps to deal with such outbreak has essentially called into question the credibility of the organization as well as the effectiveness of implementation of IHR[26]. WHO is the most important of the international groups that work to stop pandemics. It is also the legal authority which interacts with pandemics and other similar outbreaks around the world.[27] The current version of the International Human Rights Convention (IHRC) entered into force on June 15, 2007[28].

All of the abovementioned responses of WHO essentially focuses on how it has responded to many other previous pandemics. It is thereby had been expected to provide a better performance during the COVID-19 situation. It would be wrong to state that it had not improved at all but the improvement was insignificant in the light of a strong virus such as COVID-19 that did not limit its spread only to one continent or one part of the world that caused the chaos across the world for the first few months.

2.5.1 WHO Role in Combatting COVID-19

In accordance with the IHR, the WHO has set a strategy to announce a probable pandemic of PHEIC[29] on Jan. 30, 2020, and has evaluated the risk to be extremely high in China and high internationally. This declaration was made on March 11, 2020, and it was only then that it was considered to be an epidemic of the highest severity. It goes without saying that by the end of February 2020, many nations had been fully shut down and placed under a complete lockdown by government forces. Also, as of first week of March, 2020 many other European and western countries followed the path, and even the developing countries such as India and Brazil thought of imposing a full lockdown across the country[30]. Even though all the countries took their necessary methods during these chaotic times to prevent and save themselves from the COVID-19, WHO declared that they should abide by the international human rights standards. Restrictions on trade and migration were not recommended. Hence, it is not surprising that many countries, on the other hand, have failed to meet the necessary recommendations that were provided during the latter part of the pandemic[31]. However, WHO has over the duration of this ongoing pandemic, provided with various commendable steps to combat the situation that have been stated as below:

(a) **Fund for COVID-2019 affected people:** Shortly after the pandemic was announced, established a fund that would help affected people across the world. People and organizations from everywhere in the world could make contributions to the efforts of the organization as well as its partners to aid nations with the highest priorities in protecting, identifying, and reacting to the continuing outbreak of Coronavirus. The Fund's disbursement mechanism was both quick and flexible, allowing money raised through the Fund to be distributed quickly and efficiently. Statistically, it can be deducted from the official website. More than $2B has been contributed and funded to cater the needs of more than 5,00,000 people across the world till the month of July of 2020[32].

(b) **Medical Supply:** As the Organization foresaw the rise of a worldwide crisis, it launched a major effort to address acute medical supply problems in nations with insufficient infrastructure. Consequently, a task force was established within the "COVID-19 Supply Chain System" to address various COVID-19-related challenges across countries. The said establishment of the task force happened after the organization collaboration with the World Food Program on April, 2020. While this mechanism was established and developed during the year of 2009 for the purpose of supplying necessary medicines to overburden and economically weak countries, it took a greater shift during the pandemic. Supply chain hubs have been formed in various poor third world nations, including China, Belgium, Ghana, Ethiopia, as well as Malaysia. The supply chain covered more than thirty percent of the world's requirements in April & May of 2020.[33] Prior to the deployment of this method, they also previously supplied PPE and diagnostic tests to more than 120 nations.

(c) **Solidarity Trial:** Apart from the abovementioned initiatives, they had taken up the job of launching an active *Solidarity Trial* that aimed at providing for an effective treatment method for the virus and this trial essentially involved various COVID-19 researches. Also, it provided with the information of various drugs that would be effective in order to combat the severe effect during mid-2020[34].

(d) **Funds to other nations:** they had also launched and funded various countries for the purpose of getting the vaccine easily available in the market[35].

(e) **Social Media as a tool of awareness:** they had also had been extensively active on various social media platforms to inform people about the recent news of COVID-19. They also spread awareness on how anyone should be treating themselves or their close ones if they are affected by the virus. Further, WHO had announced the release of more than $9M in the aid for the third world countries[36].

2.5.2 Critical Analysis of WHO's Role during COVID-19

The epidemic has repeatedly tested the WHO's leadership & compatibility in coping with a massive pandemic. The US had criticized the deeds of WHO in length and the then US president had suspended its donation to them in the midst of a pandemic. As it has been discussed before, WHO had showed their inefficiency in dealing with the influenza outbreak in the year of 1918-1920 and it is needless to say such pattern has been repeated by their authorities during the Covid-19 outbreak as well. One of the major important criticisms was over/estimation of the threat in hand. They had received serious allegations from different countries for failing to provide with a comprehensive design of the threat at the early stage and delayed in announcing Covid-19 as a constructive pandemic. Further, WHO slow response and financial problems in relation to better IHR implementation are two major criticisms that WHO has received over the years and same has been stated during the Covid-19 crisis as well[37].

Some scholars suggested that the IHR Treaties have not resulted in a binding international law for the participating nations because of implementation & compliance challenges. International cooperation on contagious disease surveillance and pandemic protection is governed by "soft law," which is a voluntary agreement between countries and the WHO. "Soft law," despite being neither obligatory nor enforced, yet exerts a significant political impact. Due to national self-interest, this "law" is in effect. This national self-interest is why it is in existence, as it contributes to and enhances global collaboration in infectious disease response. They succeeded in creating a system for international collaboration on contagious diseases which can sustain the expanding global difficulties faced by viruses. Famous Researcher Suthar viewed sanctions and embargoes as a potential substitute for a functional IHRC.

In certain situations, the deployment of such actions may be necessary, yet these tools can be utilized for political maneuvering predicated on the concept of double standards. Hence, in order to perform better, WHO should adopt serious strategies that would provide for a better scope of their functions in the sphere of sudden outbreak or a pandemic. At first, the organization needs to be conflict free. The political biasness of it should stop if they want to be helpful during the time of conflict. The ongoing reform of WHO should not stop at any cost. It is not only their responsibility to do so but also the member states should concentrate on providing financial aids to them as well. Also, in order to WHO to work better, the member states of the organization should have better political alignment and less conflict, especially during times like Covid-19. Also, WHO should focus on creating a global fund that would provide for a better source of task force and other necessary programs at the time of a crisis in the future.

2.6 COVID-19 Outbreak and Response of Different Nations – A Comparative Study

It might seem imperative that each country should focus on complying with one universal guideline provided by WHO and that all the countries should be following a constant measure of response in order to combat the same during the time of the pandemic. But that didn't happen during the recent COVID-19 disease outbreak. But in reality, it was clear that different nations reacted to outbreak in varied contexts and that each govt. had its own plan.

The design of such public policies framed by the government in combatting the ongoing pandemic is critical to several factors[38] such as societal and cultural differences and sometimes political biasness as well. It is important to remember other minor factors that changed the course of action of different countries[39]. Also, it is pertinent to mention that different responses by different countries is not something exclusive to the COVID-19 pandemic but it has been a pattern for many other outbreaks in the past.

As it is a proven fact that COVID-19 is essentially a virus that spreads from one person to another i.e., a virus that is susceptible to human touch, the administrative authorities essentially highlighted the importance to the citizens. To understand why various nations chose different ways to respond, we'll look at two important aspects: institutional arrangements & cultural perspectives.

2.6.1 State Institutional Arrangement

During the course of addressing policy problems, institutional arrangements can be described as "the process by which a nation employs to structure better administrative force for the purpose of building public policy and information flow." All levels of the government (central and local) rely on a particular systematic formula to embrace, imply and formulate policies that would be beneficial for all levels of the organization. Members of the public, non-governmental entities, and private sector groups that aren't recognized by the govt. make up informal institutional structures.

One formal governmental arrangement is the most important way to comprehend how the govt. responds and the different ways to fight. Even within single unified states, the extent to which decentralization or centralization is more common varies. It is to be observed that a country that relies on centralized governmental authority or a nation that works through one federal government, it is easier to provide and control the citizens with rules and regulations. When authority is distributed across multiple levels of government, as it is in decentralized governments, every level of government must be transparent about the functions and responsibilities that fall under its purview.

2.6.2 Culture Orientation

Culture orientation of a nation is another means of dealing with the public policy. Culture orientation of a nation can be distinguished into loose culture and tight culture[40]. The tightness and looseness continuum of culture often relies on the social norms, social bindings, and different degree of sanctioning within the society beliefs[41]. To understand the cultural distinctions between a tight and a loose culture, it is clear that people living in a tight culture are more likely to accept government laws and interventions[42], and they place a high value on group unity[43]. Hence, tight cultured nations are more harmonious and they care for each other for the purpose of betterment of the society. This provides extreme help for the betterment of the social groups. On the other hand, the loose cultured people often try to defy the governmental rules due to their political issues and it is more likely that the loosely based cultures are not harmonious in living together.

Although there are noticeable differences between countries in terms of the strength and complexity of NPIs, there are also noticeable differences within the countries.

The "Oxford COVID-19 Government Response Tracker (OxCGRT)"[44] is an implementing measure which has been approached by Oxford in order to provide for a system that would track the ongoing curve of the recent pandemic and how different nations are handling the same. This helped immensely by gathering the information from different public sources and the same was kept on record with the Oxford university. The pattern of the information was observed by the researchers and over time, a research team at the "University of Oxford", developed a composite index that essentially indicated how different countries are responding to COVID-19 and what are the possible stringent movements that the governmental authorities of different countries have adopted.

In the composite index as prepared by Oxford and OxCGRT, it had been seen that in the course of adopting stringent measure or indices by the four countries that were selected by Oxford, namely China, Japan, Sweden and France, it was Sweden that showed the lower result in imposing loosely bound stringent measures and France showed the highest possibility to do so. Although this does not provide us with a comparative study of these countries and whether these countries perfectly implemented their governmental COVID-19 policy, this figure of Oxford states the inclination of different countries in adapting different strategies[45].

2.6.3 An Overview of Response of Western Countries during COVID-19

The COVID-19 illness outbreak has grown to worrisome proportions. In countries like the US, where more than 60% of people were at least partially vaccinated and dosages were widely available, vaccinations were first and foremost simple to obtain. As a result, people started to go back to their normal lives. However, other nations continued to be governed strictly by COVID-19 protocol, and the global problem remained far from being resolved. In Western countries, at least two out of every three citizens believed COVID-19 posed a serious threat to their country. This is true even as the global community works to deal with the next phase of the pandemic and beyond. At least half of the people in different countries said the same thing about how communicable diseases spread in general. The way people in each country saw things was different. Polls in Italy showed that eighty-four percent of people thought COVID-19 was a big danger to their nation. In Canada and Germany, eighty percent and seventy-three percent, respectively, thought the same thing about their nations. Sixty-seven percent of the people in the US took part. Individuals in every country were more likely to think that COVID-19 is a big risk than they were to think that the risk of infection in general is a big risk. The reality that most countries are still coping with the impacts on their daily lives is not a surprise to worldwide healthcare professionals. The argument was made that as long as vaccination efforts continue, developed nation's fears will fade, and that now is the time to get ready for the next global health crisis. According to Kate Dodson, Vice President for International Health policy at the UN Foundation, "*If we don't take advantage of the current situation, we risk falling into the cycle of fear and neglect that is commonly associated with infectious disease concerns.*" Doctor Mario Ramirez who was an emergency physician and a legal expert, used the Ebola epidemic of 2014 as an illustration of the nation's lack of preparedness for a health-related calamity. As per Mr. Johnson, though, since the US was spared the destruction caused by Ebola in West Africa, resources allocated to combat domestic health dangers were quickly depleted. In the Ebola outbreak, Ramirez, who worked on new hazards at the "Department of Health and Human Services", stated, "*There is an enormous amount of pressure to adapt to public opinion and the current situation.*"[46]

One thing worth noting is that the widespread impact of COVID-19 on nations doesn't seem to be connected to an increased awareness of the virus or contagious diseases in general. Adults in Spain & Italy, which were two of the early epicentres of the pandemic, were most inclined to say that COVID-19 was a major risk. However, Canadians felt the same way, even though their nation has a much lower number of deaths than either of the European nations. A separate Morning Consult survey showed that the number of people who say they won't get immunised has gone down by an average of seven percentage points over the past 2 months in 15 countries, with Russia and the US having the most people who say they won't get vaccinated. Researchers noted that the public's mood may then be affected by messages that have been spread over the past year and by how far a nation has come in its efforts to immunise its people. According to data from the Johns Hopkins University, barely six percent of Canadians are fully vaccinated, compared to roughly one in five Italians & Spaniards. The Democratic Party is more likely to consider COVID-19 and the possibility of infection as severe concerns to the US than the Republican Party.

Even though these three nations have set a larger pattern for how to cope up with the COVID-19 disease outbreak, it is essential to highlight that other Western nations have implemented comparable measures to combat the pandemic. Most of the European Countries adopted the strategy of implying decree like France did in the early February. When the COVID-19 virus first surfaced in Europe, France was Europe's lone country dealing with the problem. France was put on lockdown as soon as the first case of COVID-19 was discovered, limiting the freedom of movement of its population. The France Government declared[47] that they were at war and the situation of the pandemic was to be treated like that as well. The same approach was adopted by Italy as well and it was eventually seen that France and Italy became two countries that were worst hit by the Pandemic. This country was hit harder than China as well as other nations nearby, despite their efforts to use the decree method to cope with the pandemic.[48]

The fact is that an overwhelming majority of adults around the world—53 percent in Australia and 75 percent in Italy—believe that spreading infectious diseases is a major public health threat. Thus, according to Esther Krofah, ED of the "Milken Institute's Faster Cures" dept., the COVID-19 pandemic *"hit a chord in our collective psyche that we should be prepared for an infectious illness." "In the future, when policymakers consider how to deal with burgeoning health crises, the best way to think about this is not to take a headline-driven approach and response, but rather to build a sustainable infrastructure that, if everything works well, people actually don't care about what the potential threats are,"* Krofah stated as govts. in the U.S. try to close the discrepancies that the outbreak has demonstrated, and as the WHO calls for the creation of a worldwide pandemic treaty, there is more support for spending more money on health of public and working together better around the world. The Biden administration aims to transmit 80 million vaccination doses to other nations, including 19 million going to Covax, a global vaccine-sharing project. In addition, the administrative & political obstacles resulting from the COVID-19 pandemic will certainly recur in any future global medical emergency.

Covax, which was founded to ensure equal immunisation accessibility worldwide, also dealt with a lack of vaccine supply as a result of powerful nations like the US acquiring millions of dosages of vaccine last summer when they were still in research. *"I'm hoping that at the end of this, we'll have found a way to be more cooperative,"* Ramirez expressed his optimism. He further stated that *"however, I'm afraid that, in the realm of realpolitik, if there's another major illness epidemic, a lot of this will be thrown to the wayside. It's impossible to predict how the next epidemic will play out."* According to the following list in decreasing order, the nations that have been identified as being at risk of an unmanageable major danger are as follows:

Italy>Spain>Canada>Germany>France>United Kingdom> United States>Australia

2.6.4 Country Specific Comparative Analysis of Western Countries France's Strategy to Combat Covid-19 – The Decree Strategy

Despite the fact that mandate and decree strategy place a strong emphasis on restricting and preventing undesirable behavior of the people against their voluntary will[49], there are some differences between them. In this sense, the strategy of declaring decree in France is based on legal precedent. On January 24, 2020 after France became the first country to detect Covid-19 after China, which made it the first in the European and Western world. Despite this, the world's largest Smurf gathering and various other protests in relation to the local election took place during the March of 2020[50]. During the early pandemic situation, the citizens of French placed a strong emphasis on liberty and the continuation of daily life. The government has made proactive steps to prevent the spread of COVID-19. Because of the unprecedented speed with which the virus was spreading, France was on the verge of experiencing a serious COVID-19 eruption by the middle of March. A consequence of this shift was a shift in response strategy from one of mitigation to one of suppression in the fight against the pandemic.

President Emmanuel Macron adopted military terminology to depict the current issue in a broadcasting speech "*We are at war*". He demanded a nationwide lockdown as well. Further, he urged that in defeating COVID-19, all of French society had to work together. Both the general public and healthcare institutions were included in this effort. France's quarantine measures were in place until May 11,2020 which marked a watershed moment in the global fight against the global epidemic virus[51].

France as a nation adopted the decree strategy to combat the evil of COVID-19. France imposed restrictions of the freedom of movement of individual citizens with the decree strategy. The people were commanded to be at home and it was also declared that if anyone violates any of such commands, he/she shall be punished with heavy fine. The citizens were only permitted to move for the purpose of collecting groceries or medicines[52]. Those who left the building were needed to acquire a documented note explaining their absence. Furthermore, if the COVID-19 shutdown rules were broken, the individuals responsible can be fined a sum ranging from €135 to €3,750, depending on the seriousness of the violation. Security checks at the airport and quarantines for people travelling through the country were implemented. Major developments, as well as the closure of a number of public meeting and gathering locations, such as schools, offices, restaurants, and public transportation, were all considered illegal.

The unitary and centralized characteristic of France provided the central government with all the due powers who acted through central ministries, performed majority of the country's public functions. Once the disease outbreak spread to the whole country, the French government was able to come up with new policies to deal with it as quickly and efficiently as possible. The reaction method in France was more coercive as well as legal-based due to the French public's lax cultural context in areas of compliance and conformity.[53]

The Sweden Response Strategy to COVID-19 – The Nudge Strategy

A number of nations have used the Sweden's Nudge policy as a means of combating COVID-19 over the year. The Nudge strategy of combating Covid-19 focuses on the behaviour of the citizens and the combat style of this strategy focuses on dictating the citizen's movement. Hence, with the help of this nudge strategy[54], Sweden directed and restricted the freedom of movement amongst the citizens and imposed several restrictions to fight the spreading of the COVID-19[55]. While many countries followed the same protocol of restricting the behaviours of the citizens under limited versions, Sweden followed the Nudge strategy to a much greater degree[56].

In the particular instance of the Nudge Strategy (NS) as it was used by the Sweden Govt. It was viewed that the citizens were only allowed to move around in small areas. The Sweden authorities had not favoured imposing a full lockdown nationwide, which essentially was the response of India. The Sweden authority regarded the pandemic as a long-term undertaking[57] and policies were designed in a way to do so. Temporary ban was imposed on every other non-essential travel and several other internal movements were implemented by the authorities. While the schools, gyms shops and restaurants were closed down, the mobility on the citizen's movement was not restricted by the authorities and only a few regulations were implemented upon them. The Sweden Government provided the citizens with all kinds of social distancing norms and the citizens were advised to abode by that[58].

However, the adopted strategy of Sweden has resulted into 13,700 dead people in Sweden because of COVID-19 as of April, 2021 which has been published according to official figures. Sweden has proved to be a highly infectious zone for Covid-19 virus in Europe, with more than 606 cases per million every day (as of April, 2021) while other neighboring European countries such as Denmark has only shown a rise of 112/115 cases per million every day[59]. By April 15, 2021, it was thought that the 75 to 100 percent of all cases in Sweden being caused by the UK SARS-Cov-2 variant.

Due to the NS of Sweden, indications have been provided by various other global authorities that there are chances that the disease will spread more quickly, causing more deaths, and affecting a greater number of young people. In some areas, intensive care units are already at capacity. It had been seen during the second wave Sweden had chosen their Nudge strategy to combat COVID-19. As when all other countries in April, 2021 shut down all their public places, Sweden slowly paced up. Despite the influx of cases of COVID-19 in Sweden, the high schools had opened up in Sweden since April of 2021. Such action of the government has essentially raised the eyebrows of WHO on the matters of accountability, ethics and governance.

On the contrary, there had been other researches[60] that show a quite successful implication of Sweden in complying with the *Nudge Strategy* as it essentially kept a balance between the economic conditions of the country and provided necessary public policy strategy for the citizens as a whole[61].

2.6.5 An Overview of Asian Countries

A report by the Organization for Economic Co-operation and Development (OECD) found that Australia, Korea, Japan, New Zealand outperformed the majority of countries in reducing the impact of COVID-19 on healthcare systems in Asia-Pacific countries and in responding to COVID-19 in the first wave of the pandemic infection. There is a lot of trust & commitment to social distance in these countries. They also have rigorous testing, tracking, & isolation systems. Many nations, such as Thailand and Vietnam, have proved the importance of adopting a proactive strategy in order to effectively manage the virus and reduce fatalities. A Quick Look at Your Health It is estimated that COVID-19 has been responsible for around 140,300 deaths in the Asia-Pacific countries, accounting for approximately 12 percent of all recorded deaths worldwide as of the beginning of October 2020. Person's life was severely impacted by the virus' rapid spread in a number of nations notably Philippines & Indonesia. As a safety measure, govts. should discuss potential risks, build responsive surge capacity, increase the number of people working in health care, and then use digital health technology to its full potential before vaccines are commonly accessible. Low & middle-income countries in Asia required to improve their healthcare costs even before the economic crisis. As the pandemic continues, it is imperative that the already limited resources are not diverted from important medical services. This holds true throughout and during the outbreak. Due to their limited resources as well as dependence on consumer discretionary spending, it is probable that these countries' financial capacity will not be sufficient to meet the substantial expenses of the COVID-19 response. Since the pandemic started, services for preventing and treating cancer, heart disease, diabetes, HIV, tuberculosis, and malaria have been severely disrupted. It is also important to remember that COVID-19 has big indirect effects on pregnant women, infants, young kids, and teens. Although life expectancy has gone up by six years since two thousand, reaching seventy in 2018, maternal morbidity in lower-middle as well as lower-income Asia-Pacific nations is still more than twice the "Sustainable Development Goals (SDGs)" target. Infant mortality is still seven times higher in low- and lower-middle-income Asia-Pacific countries than in high-income Asia-Pacific countries and the OECD average. The SDG target of 12 fatalities per 1,000 persons has been surpassed by this rate (as of 2018).[62]

The majority of health spending in lower-middle and lower-income nations is accounted for by payments paid by households out of their own pockets. In 2017, patients in Cambodia, Bangladesh, Pakistan, India, and Myanmar paid more than 60 cents of every dollar spent on health care "out of pocket." Because of Confucius's legacy, Asian nations like Japan & China are usually thought of as having close-knit cultures. During the COVID-19 crisis, a general societal consensus has been reached in these countries regarding the necessity of complying with the containment and closure measures[63]. On the other hand, a loosely knit society or culture often shows the pattern of non-harmonious settings where people have low tolerance for one another and the behavioural pattern of such cultural group essentially depends on the individual's preferences[64]. Hence, *independence and more self-contained cultures are often categorized as loosely knit cultures such as France and so more stringent measures are always needed.*

2.6.6 Country Specific Comparative Analysis of Asian Countries China's Response to COVID-19 Pandemic – The Mandate Strategy

In contrast to Sweden's reaction method, China's COVID-19 response is mediated by the usage of authority-based coercive forces in combination with societal agreement.[65] The Chinese authorities mobilised the public across the country by invoking wartime narratives and emphasising the importance of group solidarity to bring down the dissemination of COVID-19. In reaction to COVID-19, the Chinese govt. instituted a lockdown across the country's largest cities, as well as an obligatory social distance policy for all citizens. During the lockdown, all of the people who lived there had to stay at home. The power to monitor the behaviour of residents was delegated by the state to large grassroots community-based organisations with widespread support[66]. In a recent conference, the WHO executive director, Mike Ryan has essentially congratulated China for managing their Corona cases and also stated, *".....deepest congratulations...to the front-line health workers in China and the population who worked together tirelessly to bring the disease to this very low level."* Even though China had been the source of COVID-19, it had regulated a well monitored system for responding to epidemics. The SARS-CoV virus and its related high fatality rate are still prominent in the thoughts of the most of adult Chinese citizens. "*The society was extremely concerned about what could happen in the event of a corona virus outbreak*," Xi Chen said. "*Other countries do not have such recent memories of a pandemic,* ". They're more capable of living with their kids than to live alone but close to them as they become older[67]. Even though just 3 percent of the Chinese population resides in nursing homes, these services have been recognized as crucial sources of contamination in various western nations. [68]

The administration authorities had been investing in high-tech tracking systems that are cutting-edge in their design. The health code colour system used in the smartphone application, for example, categorization of individuals into three groups that would track their recent health and their recent travel histories whatsoever. Afterwards, the system shall determine whether or not the monitored people need to be quarantined or not. Additionally, the utilization of street cameras to catch those without masks as well as detect those with indications of sickness has been helpful in disease regulation and monitoring[69].

Japan's Strategy to combat COVID-19 – The Boost Strategy

In accordance to Sweden, Japan did not provide for a strict measure of lockdown or city blockade and strictly adhered to the boost strategy of combatting COVID-19 where the Japanese Government provided for several policies that would enlighten the citizens of Japan with the updated rules and regulations of COVID-19 and its restrictions[70]. The Japanese Govt. issued the *"Basic Policies for Novel Coronavirus Disease Control"* on 25th Feb, 2020 and the same has been updated more than five times till today. The Japanese Government issued a state emergency and provided for special restrictions in different provinces such as Saitama, Tokyo, Kanagawa and Osaka. The boost strategy of Japan adopted three methods which would guide the disease in a way that the citizens would not need to be confined in their homes for weeks and months. At first, they had the strategy of early detection of the disease through rapid COVID-19 test. Japanese Government implemented home to home tests within a few weeks of outbreak of the same. Secondly, the government of Japan provided for extensive healthcare & legislation which helped extensively in combatting the

COVID-19 with great results. Thirdly, the Japanese Government[71] established better medical services and behavioral modification of the general population as a last resort to provide better guidance and standards that would limit the future spread of COVID-19 disease[72].

Thus, it is evident from Japan's strategy to combat COVID-19 is to go for rapid vaccination process and rapid testing procedure. The boost strategy of Japan was first implied on the old population first. Japan government had been extremely clear with their intention to provide for their vaccination procedure with old-young-middle scheme. With such procedure, Japan succeeded at preventing COVID-19 at a much higher and faster rate than any other countries at all times. From research[73], it can be seen that this strategy of Japan essentially helped in minimizing the window of rapid death and treating more people to recovery.

During the first half or the first wave of COVID-19, Japan faced with serious issues such as the health care capacity, cross border transportation issue and other public health sector related issues. It is pertinent to mention that Japan had faced with such issues due to the occurrence of multiple interventions which were not sufficiently harmonized at the administrative level and all the discussion and communication to such effect fell into deaf ear[74]. It is true that Japan successfully kicked back the first wave of COVID-19 at a very initial stage of 2020. But the same did not stay with Japan and slowly Japan had to answer the economical and epidemiological consequences of COVID-19. The infections which included skin irritation accompanied Japan in its latter stage of COVID-19. It will be necessary to examine previous responses in order to determine the root causes of problems. COVID-19 will benefit from not only collecting successful responses, but also shall change its course of path by collecting the previous mistakes of the governmental authorities including WHO. As a result, the global approach to COVID-19 will be continually improved.

A Critical Study of Indian Strategy of dealing with COVID-19

COVID-19 came in India around the end of March 2020, after spreading across most of Asia and Europe, with most countries taking proper action. During this time, the Indian Government tried to follow the modern western rule of dealing with Covid-19, essentially the Decree method adopted by France and Italy but India did not consider the many factors in its way. While the Decree method was adopted by France and Italy that had comparatively lesser population density across the country and lesser young population[75]. India was composed of different factors and characteristics. The Indian government's significant move to put a lockdown on the whole country really messed up the lives of the people, and for those living in extreme poverty, it became a fight for life or death. The sudden halt of every transportation system caused a great panic across the country and all the workers from different parts of India started to migrate from their place of work to the place of residence. Millions of migrant workers walked thousands of kilometres to reach their home in order to provide some food for themselves and among all these chaos, the Indian Government failed to do something in their aid[76].

On top of that, Indian government tried to implement several other strategies on top of nation-wide lockdown such as the boost strategy of Japan during the 2nd wave of COVID-19 and the mandate strategy of China as well. However, the mix of every other strategy only created a great confusion amongst the citizens. Further, the lack of adequate measures and means of implementing the due recourse of the pandemic strategies made it exceedingly difficult for the citizens of the county[77]. While the nation-wide lockdown showed a great promise that India might be the first country to restrict the spread of COVID-19 with such a huge population, it was not the case and the same was detected in the 2nd wave of the COVID-19. The disrupted strategies of Indian Govt. necessarily weakened the economics, confused the general public and disrupted the lifestyles of many poor workers by leaving them jobless[78].

2.6.7 An Overview of Response of African Countries

As of Sept. 13, 2020, thirty-five African nations confirmed widespread transmission, eleven confirmed groups, and three confirmed sporadic cases. There were 1,412,699 occurrences, 34,077 fatalities, as well as a "Case Fatality Rate (CFR)" of 2.4 per cent in Africa as of Sept. 22, 2020, as per the continent's "Centers for Disease Control and Prevention (CDC)". [79] The most cases have been found in Northern Africa (forty-six percent), abided by the Southern Hemisphere (thirty percent), Western Africa (seven percent), Eastern Africa (fifteen percent), as well as Central Africa (one percent). On September 15th,

2020, South Africa had reported 21% of all cases, Morocco 27%, Ethiopia 10%, Libya 9%, Tunisia 4%, and Algeria 4%. These countries accounted for more than 75% of all cases in the country.[80] On the 16th of September, 2020, just fewer than 5,000 cases of COVID-19 had been confirmed in 25 African countries, while between 5,000 and 10,000 cases had been confirmed in nine African countries as of the time of this writing (on Sept. 16, 2020). As of Sept. 16, 2020, thirty-four African nations had identified fewer than 10,000 COVID-19 infections collectively. Only thirteen nations have reported more than 10,000 cases. Africa reported[81] a total of 41,936 illnesses among healthcare professionals between the 25th of February and the 8th of September in the year 2020. In recent years, several nations have achieved significant progress in decreasing poverty, improving indices of the healthcare system, and enhancing the effectiveness of government. The "African Continental Free Trade Area (AfCFTA)" was designed to spur economic growth across the continent, which, according to forecasts, will have a combined GDP of over US$3.4 trillion by the time it takes effect on July 1, 2020. But the epidemic has prompted the start date to be pushed back, particularly in light of the cancellation of the African Union (AU) Summit in May 2020, which was scheduled to take place in Addis Ababa, Ethiopia. The African Union Commission has suggested a new preliminary start date for commerce under the AfCFTA of January 1, 2021, as recommended by the African Union Commission. The first recorded incidence of COVID-19 on the continent occurred in Egypt around the middle of February 2020. The WHO says that, right now, at first, the countries were spared the worst effects of the virus's spread. This was because they didn't have as many air links with the entire world, particularly with China & Europe. Since then, however, the number of reported cases has progressively climbed. *"Anywhere between 300,000 and 3.3 million African people might lose their lives as a direct result of COVID-19,"* as per "United Nations Economic Commission for Africa (UNECA)" assessment published in Apr. 2020.

Many African countries followed the same approach of implementing decree strategy for the purpose of dealing with the first wave of the COVID-19. While the same worked for the first time, all the system broke loose by the time of the second wave and most of the countries of Africa were severely affected by the severity of the virus by the end of September or October, 2020.

2.7 Conclusion

Comparing the four major nations which kept their COVID-19 instances under control during the 1st and 2nd waves of the disease outbreak, India is definitely one of the countries which is still experiencing difficulties. Being the second highest country with COVID-19 cases, India has already faced with the critical conditions of death wave and the continuous uprising surge of cases is concerning[82]. Even though the low case-fatality in India is somewhat reassuring as India has more young people in its age group than old people, India still resides at a warned phase. Indian citizens are getting their vaccination rapidly and the boost strategy as followed by Japan is slowly and steadily has been embraced in India. It can be predicted that India might have escaped the death trap of the 3rd wave of the pandemic but it is still at a developing stage and no conclusive result in comparison to other countries can be provided in this thesis whatsoever.

Footnotes

1 47, Ghosh, Jayati – "*A critique of the Indian government's response to the COVID-19 pandemic.*" 519-530, J.I.B.E., (2020).

2 Ibid

3 Anjum R. Faisal, Anam. Sidra, Rahman. Sajjad –"*Novel Coronavirus disease 2019 (COVID-19): new challenges and new responsibilities in developing countries.*" NATIONAL LIBRARY OF MEDICINE (Sept. 10th 2021, 9:38 AM), https://www.ncbi.nlm.nih.gov/pmc/articles/PMC7644207.

4 UN General Assembly, Entry into force of the constitution of the World Health Organization, 17 November 1947, A/RES/131, available at: https://www.refworld.org/docid/3b00f09554.html [accessed 17 August 2022]

5 UN General Assembly, Transforming our world : the 2030 Agenda for Sustainable Development, 21 October 2015, A/RES/

70/1, available at: https://www.refworld.org/docid/57b6e3e44.html [accessed 17 August 2022]

6 The Office of the High Commissioner for Human Rights published a report entitled Implementing the United Nations "Protect, Respect, and Remedy" Framework, which was published in Geneva. Business and human rights concepts that should be followed 2011: The Office of the High Commissioner for Human Rights published a report entitled Implementing the United Nations "Protect, Respect, and Remedy" Framework, which was published in Geneva.

7 Yamin AE.- "*Transformative combinations: women's health and human rights*." J.A.W.A, (1972).

8 Link BG and Phelan J. "*Social conditions as fundamental causes of disease*". J.H.S.B (1995).

9 Marnot M & Willinkson RC- Social Determinants of Health (Oxford University Press, 1999).

10 UDHR stands for the Universal Declaration of Human Rights. Resolution 217 A of the General Assembly of the United Nations (III). The United Nations published this book in 1948 in New York, New York.

11 Craven M- the International Covenant on Economic, Social and Cultural Rights: A Perspective on its Development. (Clanderon Press, 1995).

12 ICESCR is an acronym that stands for International Covenant on Economic, Social, and Cultural Rights (International Covenant on Economic, Social, and Cultural Rights). The United Nations released this book in New York, New York, in 1966, and it is still in print today. The United Nations document A/6316 is available online.

13 The Constitution of the World Health Organization. The World Health Organization was established in Geneva, Switzerland, in 1946.

14 The International Convention on the Elimination of All Forms of Racial Discrimination (International Convention on the Elimination of All Forms of Racial Discrimination) (International

Convention on the Elimination of All Forms of Racial Discrimination). The United Nations released this book in New York, New York, in 1966, and it is still in print today. The paper A/6014 is from the United Nations.

15 Traditional indigenous and tribal peoples living within sovereign states have their rights safeguarded under the International Convention on the Rights of Indigenous and Tribal Peoples in Independent Countries (Convention 169). In 1989, the International Labor Organization (ILO) was created in Geneva, Switzerland, as a non-governmental organisation.

16 Women's rights are protected by the United Nations' Committee on the Elimination of Discrimination Against Women (UN Women). The subject of General Recommendation No. 24 is the health of women and girls. The year is 1999, and Geneva, Switzerland is the setting.

17 Christensen, T., Lægreid, P., Rykkja, L. H. (2016). *Organizing for crisis management: Building governance capacity and legitimacy.* Public Administration Review, 76(6), 887–897.

18 Ibid

19 76 (2), Carayannopoulos, G. Whole of government:- *The solution to managing crises*? 76(2), 251–265, A.J.P.A.(2017)

20 Jessop, B. - *Redesigning the state, reorienting state power, and rethinking the state. In Leicht, K. T., Jenkins, J. C. (Eds.)*, pp. 41–61, H.O.P. (2010).

21 Coccia M. Factors determining the diffusion of COVID-19 and suggested strategy to prevent future accelerated viral infectivity similar to COVID. https://doi.org/10.1016/j.scitotenv.2020.138474 , (LAST VISITED ON Sept. 7, 2021)

22 Bhadra, A., Mukherjee, A., & Sarkar, K. *Impact of population density on Covid-19 infected and mortality rate in India.* Modeling earth systems and environment, 1–7, A.O.P., (2020).

23 17, Sandra C. Melvin. Et al- *The Role of Public Health in COVID-19 Emergency Response Efforts From a Rural Health Perspective.* CENTRE FOR DISEASE CONTROL

AND PREVENTION (July 23rd, 2017), https://www.cdc.gov/pcd/issues/2020/20_0256.htm.

24 Kuznetsova,Lidia -*COVID-19: The World Community Expects the World Health Organization to Play a Stronger Leadership and Coordination Role in Pandemics Control,* FRONTIERS (Sept. 8, 2020) https://www.frontiersin.org/articles/10.3389/fpubh.2020.00470/full.

25 Ibid

26 Burkle F.*Global Health security demands a strong international health regulations treaty and leadership from a highly resourced World Health Organization.*Disaster Med Public Health Prepared. (2015).

27 Supra Note 14

28 A World at Risk: Annual Report on Global Preparedness for Health Emergencies, Geneva, World Health Organization., https://reliefweb.int/report/world/world-risk-annual-report-global-preparedness-health-emergencies-global-preparedness?gclid=Cj0KCQjwlemWBhDUARIsAFp1rLXCjvZcX9NFAS9ysozSIWMQOwpqjIaiwa4f3xAI4Ni05bkuQBqmVJsaAkNSEALw_wcB,(Last accessed on 11th Oct. 2021, 2:30 pm).

29 Public Health Emergency of International Concern

30 Habibi R, Burci GL, de Campos TC, Chirwa D, Cinà M, Dagron S,*et al. Do not violate the international health regulations during the COVID-19 outbreak.*LANCET (2020).

31 Gostin LO.*COVID-19 reveals urgent need to strengthen the World Health Organization.* JAMA. (2020).

32 Ibid

33 Timeline of WHO's Response to COVID 19, https://www.who.int/news-room/detail/29-06-2020-covidtimeline (Last accessed Nov 10, 2021)

34 WHO- SOLIDARITY FOR CLINICAL TRIALS, https://www.who.int/emergencies/diseases/novel-coronavirus-2019/global-research-on-novel-coronavirus-2019-ncov/solidarity-

clinical-trial-for-covid-19-treatments (last accessed on Nov 10, 2021)

35 WHO- Contingency Fund for Emergency - https: // www.who.int/emergencies/funding/contingency-fund-for-emergencies (last accessed on Nov 10, 2021)

36 WHO Timeline COVID 19, - https://www.who.int/news-room/detail/27-04-2020-who-timeline—covid-19 (Last accessed on Nov 10 2021)

37 Habibi R, Burci GL, de Campos TC, Chirwa D, Cinà M, Dagron S, et al. *Do not violate the international health regulations during the COVID-19 outbreak.* LANCET (2020)

38 Geva-May, I. *Cultural theory: The neglected variable in the craft of policy analysis.* 243–265, J.C.P.A. (2002).

39 Berkman, A., Garcia, J., Muñoz-Laboy, M., Paiva, V., Parker, R. - *A critical analysis of the Brazilian response to HIV/AIDS: Lessons learned for controlling and mitigating the epidemic in developing countries.* A.J.P.H., (2005)

40 Hofstede, G., Hofstede, G. J., Minkov, M. (2010). Cultures and organizations: Software for the mind (3rd ed, 2010).

41 Gelfand, M. J.*et al. Differences between tight and loose cultures: A 33-nation study.* SCIENCE (2011).

42 Gaenslen, F. *Culture and decision making in China, Japan, Russia, and the United States.* WORLD POLITICS (1986).

43 Ibid

44 Hale, T., Angrist, N., Kira, B., Petherick, A., Phillips, T., Webster, S. - *Variation in government responses to Covid-19 Version 5.0.* O.U.P. (2020).

45 Yan, B., Zhang, X., Wu, L., Zhu, H., & Chen, B. - *Why Do Countries Respond Differently to COVID-19? A Comparative Study of Sweden, China, France, and Japan.* A.R.P.A. (2020)

46 Gaby Galvin0 Western Countries View COVID 19 and the Spread of Infectious Diseases as Major Threat 2021 At:- https://morningconsult.com/2021/06/10/global-health-covid-infectious-diseases-threat-poll/ (Last accessed on Oct, 12, 2021).

47 Wollmann, H. *Local government reforms in Great Britain, Sweden, Germany and France: Between multi-function and single-purpose organisations.* L.G.S. (2010)..

48 Nasir, K. M., Turner, B. S. - *Governing as gardening: Reflections on soft authoritarianism in Singapore.* (2013).

49 Keeler, J. T. S. - *Opening the window for reform: Mandates, crises, and extraordinary policy-making.* C.P.S. (1993)/

50 Yan, B., Zhang, X., Wu, L., Zhu, H., & Chen, B. -*Why Do Countries Respond Differently to COVID-19? A Comparative Study of Sweden, China, France, and Japan.* A.R.P.A. (2020).

51 Ibid

52 Supra 70

53 Ibid

54 Hertwig, R., Grüne-Yanoff, T. - *Nudging and boosting: Steering or empowering good decisions.* P.P.S. (2017).

55 Claeson M, Hanson S - *COVID-19 and the Swedish enigma***.** LANCET (2020).

56 Ibid

57 Swedish Foreign Minister Ann Linde believes that the country's coronavirus response has been pragmatic, not libertarian. https://www.politico.eu/article/sweden-coronavirus-leader-ann-linde-defends-approach-shrugs-off-far-right-embrace/ (LST ACCESSED ON OCt, 12, 2021.)

58 Nygren, K. G., Olofsson, A. - Managing the COVID-19 pandemic through individual responsibility: The consequences of a world risk society and enhanced ethopolitics. J.R.R. (2020).

59 Hannah Ritchie, Edouard Mathieu, Lucas Rodés-Guirao, Cameron Appel, Charlie Giattino, Esteban Ortiz-Ospina, Joe Hasell, Bobbie Macdonald, Diana Beltekian and Max Roser (2020) - "Coronavirus Pandemic (COVID-19)". OurWorldInData.org. (Last accessed on Oct, 12th, 2021).

60 Mishra, S., Scott, J.A., Laydon, D.J.et al -Comparing the responses of the UK, Sweden and Denmark to COVID-19 using counterfactual modelling. Sci Rep (2021).

61 Flaxman, S.et al- *Estimating the effects of non-pharmaceutical interventions on COVID-19 in Europe.* NATURE (2020).

62 OECD- "Asia-Pacific countries have managed COVID-19 crisis relatively well but major challenges remain in low-middle-income countries" https://www.oecd.org/china/asia-pacific-countries-have-managed-covid-19-crisis-relatively-well-but-major-challenges-remain-in-low-middle-income-countries.htm.(Last accessed on Nov. 10,2021).

63 Gelfand, M. J. -. Culture's constraints: International differences in the strength of social norms. P.S., (2012).

64 Markus, H., Kitayama, S. - *Culture and the self: Implications for cognition, emotion, and motivation.* P.R. (1991)

65 Kraemer, M. U. G., Yang, C.-H., Gutierrez, B., Wu, C.-H., Klein, B., Pigott, D. M., Scarpino, S. V. - *The effect of human mobility and control measures on the COVID-19 epidemic in China. Science*, (2020).

66 Zhang, S., *et al - COVID-19 containment: China provides important lessons for global response.* FRONTIERS (2020).

67 AlTakarli N.S. - *China's Response to the COVID-19 Outbreak: A Model for Epidemic Preparedness and Management.* D.M.J. (2020)

68 Burki, Talha - *China's successful control of COVID-19.* LANCET (2020).

69 AlTakarli N.S. - *China's Response to the COVID-19 Outbreak: A Model for Epidemic Preparedness and Management.* D.M.J. (2020).

70 Bradt, J. (2019). *Comparing the effects of behaviorally informed interventions on flood insurance demand: An experimental analysis of "boosts" and " nudges."* A.O.P. (2019).

71 Hayasaki, E. - *Covid-19: How Japan squandered its early jump on the pandemic.* BMJ (2020).

72 Jacobs, A. J.- *Devolving authority and expanding autonomy in Japanese prefectures and municipalities.* GOVERNANCE (2003).

73 Sunohara S, Asakura T, Kimura T, Ozawa S, Oshima S, Yamauchi D, et al.- *Effective vaccine allocation strategies, balancing economy with infection control against COVID-19 in Japan.*PLOS ONE (2021).

74 Shimizu K, Negita M -*Lessons Learned from Japan's Response to the First Wave of COVID-19: A Content Analysis,* (2021).

75 Supra Note 16

76 Ghosh, J. *"A critique of the Indian government's response to the COVID-19 pandemic."* J. IND. BUS ECON (2020)

77 M.Z.M.Noman, Mohammad Rauf, Zubair Ahmed, Tarique Faiyaz, Saif A.Khan& Madiha Tahreem. "*Quarantine Law Enforcement & Corona Virus(COVID-19) Pandemic in India*" J.X.U. (2020).

78 Shamasunder, Sriram, et al. "*COVID-19 reveals weak health systems by design: why we must re-make global health in this historic moment.*" G.P.H. (2020).

79 It is critical to distinguish between debt cancellations, debt service, and debt standstill or moratorium. Debt cancellations are different from debt service. What Africa requires is a debt moratorium before any discussions aboutdebt reductions can take place. Africa's debt may be split into three categories: multilateral debt, which is owing to international organisations such as the International Monetary Fund and the World Bank; bilateral debt; and commercial debt. Commercialdebt, with a total value of around US$17 billion, is the greatest component in terms of scale.

80 In the long run, the benefits of the AfCFTA are anticipated to accrue throughout all African nations, regardless of their geographical location. AfCFTA success depends on African

countries working together to eliminate non-tariff barriers such as import bans, discriminatory rules of origin, quality conditions imposed by an importer on an exporter, complex regulatory environments, general or product-specific tariffs, unjustified sanitary and phytosanitary conditions, and the establishment of a minimum import price for goods entering their countries from other countries.

81 Africa Centres for Disease Control and Prevention, "New report provides African governments real-time information and guidance to find the balance in COVID-19 response," Africa Centres for Disease Control and Prevention-https://africacdc.org/news-item/new-report-provides-african-governments-real-time-information-and-guidance-to-find- the balance-in-covid-19- response/, (Last Accessed on Nov., 8, 2021).

82 Pal, R., & Yadav, U. (2020). *COVID-19 Pandemic in India: Present Scenario and a Steep Climb Ahead.* Journal of primary care & community health, 11, 2150132720939402. https://doi.org/10.1177/2150132720939402

03
CHAPTER

LEGAL DIMENSION OF COVID-19 IN INDIA

3.1 Background

Since its inception, human society has endured a number of disasters. These man-made and natural disasters have put human survival to the test several times, and they have played a significant part in the molding of nearly every facet of human existence throughout recent history. Droughts and pandemics, as well as man-made challenges such as the two world wars and the bombing of Hiroshima and Nagasaki, have all had an impact on every segment of human civilization on a global scale, or at the very least at international and national levels. The effects of these have made human understand the mediocrity of his or her existence on this planet, and they have done so in both predictable and unforeseen ways. Recent incidents involving the worldwide transmission of COVID-19 are a good example of these kinds of disasters.

3.2 Introduction

A public health strategy that complied with Indian laws and policies was developed by the Indian government as a result of the new COVID-19. All state governments began adhering to the "Epidemic Diseases Act (EDA) of 1897" on March 11, 2020. Which simply meant that there would be a voluntary curfew for the whole population and that people would have to avoid any sort of physical contact outside their premises.

The devastating effect of the virus was referred to as a calamity because people believed the community couldn't handle it and that emergency measures were required. The public health system and equipment faced an unprecedented challenge during the pandemic, putting a variety of health standards to the test. Sections 188[1], 269[2], 270[3], and 271[4] of the penal code from 1860, as well as Sec. 144 of the Criminal Procedure Code of 1973[5], were used to impose the lockdown. In order to effectively regulate the terrifying new virus, it was necessary to do a thorough analysis of both the IPC of 1860 and the EDA of 1897. These laws were passed 160 and 123 years ago, respectively, making them both relatively ancient. With the assistance of these two legislations alongside Sec. 6[6], 10[7], 38,[8] & 72[9] of the Disaster Management Act (DMA), 2005, lockdowns were implemented across the country in three stages: I (25th Mar., 2020 to 14th Apr. 14, 2020), II (15th Apr., 2020 to 3rd May, 2020), & III (4th May, 2019 to 17th May, 2020).

This chapter is essential because it is the core heart of the research. It focuses on the role of the Disaster Management Act 2005, the Epidemic Diseases Act of 1897 Alias Epidemic Diseases (Amendment) Act, 2020, and other relevant legislative imperatives that were implemented to control the spread and adversities as caused by COVID-19 calamity. As part of a cooperative federalism approach, the power, structure, and operation of disaster management agencies at all levels of government shall be reviewed in this chapter. Additionally, it will discuss the "Public Health Mission (Prevention, Management, Control, Pandemics, Bio-Terrorism, and Disasters) Bill," which was introduced in 2017 and later amended in 2022 to better fit its necessary outcome and contributory role to the present pandemic crisis.

3.3 The Indian Legal System and Constitutional Framework with Respect to Health- Emergencies

With its preamble and 448 articles incorporated in 25 parts, the Indian Constitution has been deemed the world's longest constitution. In addition, there are twelve schedules. Since its adoption on November 26, 1949, the constitution has undergone many amendments. After the announcement of independence, the country was designated as a "sovereign, socialist, secular, democratic republic" that guarantees "justice, liberty, equality, and brotherhood" to all of its citizens. Parliament and state legislatures are endowed with the duty of formulating rules and regulations as well as laws into the form of codified legislation, debate over it, and enact it, after which it is implemented in conformity with the wider principles set out above. In this way of thinking, it is the state's main job to protect the lives of its citizens in case of unplanned events or natural catastrophes. This chapter will now be divided into two parts majorly. The first focuses on the health-related provisions of the Indian Constitution, while the second examines the numerous laws that the Indian government established during the outbreak, including the Epidemic Diseases Act, 1897 (EDA) and the Disaster Management Act, 2005 (DMA).[10]

3.3.1 Constitutional Provisions Pertaining to Health

The legal and constitutional foundations for dealing with outbreaks came under scrutiny as soon as the statewide lockdown orders were issued, both within and outside of the country. Everyone in India, without exception, has a right to health. Art. 21[11] expressly states that every citizen has a fundamental right to life & personal liberty, which may have been violated when the nation-imposed a thorough state-wide lockdown. There are healthcare initiatives in Part IV that adhere to the "Directive Principles for State Policy". Art. 39(a)[12] specifies that it is the role of the state to provide citizens with security by safeguarding the "Right to an Adequate Means of Subsistence." In accordance with the rules that are incorporated within Art. 41[13] the fundamental purpose of the government is to "provide public assistance in the circumstances of unemployment, old age, disease, and disablement." In compliance with Art. 42[14], a maternity benefit is offered, which provides "protection of the infant's and mother's health." Article 47[15] is concerned with "increasing people's diet and living standards, as well as the general health of the population." An overall twenty-eight states & eight UTs make up the country of India. An important contrast exists between the operating rights and obligations of the federal government as opposed to those of states and territories, as stipulated by the Constitution.

According to Art. 246[16], the UTs as well as the States are divided into seven schedules, each of which can be amended. The 7th Schedule includes the Union List, State List, as well as Concurrent List. The union list has 97 items that center has power to make laws, whereas the state list contains 62 items that are adhere by state governments. The concurrent list has 52 subjects over which both Parliament as well as state governments have authority. In the event of a disagreement, the Constitution gives the federal government authority over matters that are included in the concurrent list. Public health legislation can be adopted either by the central government or by the states individually. The Indian Constitution includes public health-related issues on all three lists. The union list numbers 28 and 81 belong to quarantine, which incorporates all issues related to seamen's hospitals and maritime medical institutions. Under the sixth item on the state list, states can pass laws about "healthcare, sanitation, hospitals, dispensaries, and preventing animal diseases." Item twenty-nine of concurrent list allows for the creation of legislation that deal with the healthcare profession and the control of communicable or infectious illnesses and pests impacting humans, animals, and plants from spreading from one state to the other. This recommendation was made by a "High-Level Group" for the healthcare[17] system that was established by the "Fifteenth Finance Commission"[18] Including the "Right to Health" as a fundamental right was also advocated.

After doing a more in-depth fundamental analysis of the Indian Constitution, it has become abundantly evident that neither the explicit recognition nor the direct recognition of the right to health as a fundamental right has been included. Although the drafters as well as the founding fathers had a big picture in mind, they gave the duty to the state in the form of "Directive Principles of State Policy" in Part IV. This part of the Constitution declares that the state is accountable for ensuring that its citizens have social & economic justice. It has some impact on public health policy, whether directly or via indirect action, as a whole. State duty for keeping the peace in order to encourage the general public health and well-being is established in Art. 38[19].

The President of India is given the power to declare financial, state, and national emergencies. A "national emergency" is declared when war, an external invasion, or a violent rebellion endanger the safety of the country, but there is no mention of a medical emergency whatsoever. Although imprisoning people or maintaining strict controls to stop the spread of infection currently affects their basic rights in a way that is contrary to the interests of citizens, several constitutional practices have been examined multiple times, and even more so during COVID-19, along with ample consultations with various stakeholders to cover medical cases in emergency provisions.[20] Following the realization that the outbreak constituted a serious crisis with wide-ranging national ramifications, the Union and the States were faced with the question of what constitutional measures may be employed to respond. Even if some intellectuals questioned the Constitution's constitutionality in emergency situations, others questioned whether the national government is best suited to make key decisions about pandemic control and management. This was further emphasised by a decision in the case of "Paschim Banga Ket Mazdoor Samity,"[21] in which the court decided that the government's role is to provide all citizens with medical care and to strive for the public's well-being. For the state's part, Art. 21 states that it is responsible for protecting and preserving the rights of its citizens. According to another landmark judgment, the right to good health extends beyond the absence of disease. Employers can use health and medical services to help motivate their workers to work at their peak physical and mental capacities. To summarise, medical facilities are considered to be a component of social security.[22] In the matter of "T. Ramakrishna Rao"[23], the Hon'ble High Court made the comment that maintaining the environment is a responsibility shared by both citizens and the government. Art. 21[24] also talks about protecting and preserving the environment. People's health and safety are the state's primary responsibilities under Article 47[25], and this obligation must be enforced against any government organization or authority, no matter how wealthy it may be. The Ratlam Municipal Corporation case is a well-known example of the upholding this principle. [26] The notion of "personal freedom" is intended to contain rights which may or may not be highly correlated to a person's life and freedom; this includes the right to health. During the landmark judgement of Hon'ble apex court in "Keshvananda Bharti Case"[27] the commencement of the phase of progressive jurisprudence after the recognition of fundamental rights was signaled. In addition, the established regulations for the promotion of Public Interest Limited as well as access to the courts were reduced during the same time period. This has led to a significant increase in the number of health-related court proceedings. Subsequently, there have been additional changes, such as the formation of consumer forums and the recent acknowledgement of healthcare as a fundamental health regulation. This is due to the fact that the apex court decided, in the first place, to keep the public's ability to directly approach it open for the sake of the protection. This choice has led to the current predicament that we find ourselves in.

This right to life and liberty is protected by Article 21, which many people think involves more than just the right to live. In the case of "Pt. Parmanand Katara vs Union of India[28]," the Supreme Court of India ruled that medical professionals are responsible for public health and have an underlying obligation to safeguard it. This is so that those who are innocent can be kept safe, and those who are accused can be penalized. In the case of, "Spring Meadow Hospital", the court concluded that individuals who are associated with the formation of pertinent laws require a deeper level of education regarding the specifics of the right to health. The adoption of laws that address the ethical and legal issues surrounding the commercialization of organ transplantation has been crucial in making the right to health a reality. In the end, the recognition of human dignity as well as the right to health has led to a greater appreciation for health. In yet another scenario, "Bandhua Mukti Morcha vs. Union of India"[29], the court said that the "Directive Principles of State Policy" are influential, but the state should follow them. In "Consumer Education and Research Centre vs. Union of India", the Supreme Court stated that the right to health was fundamental to living a meaningful life and executing the right to life under Part III[30]. The court also said that being healthy means having access to healthcare treatment so that you can have the best quality of life possible.

But the Indian constitution does not have a clause for a "health emergency." The President of India can announce national, state, as well as financial emergency situations. When the nation's safety is in danger because of war, foreign threats, or armed insurgency, a national emergency is announced. If the state's constitution falls apart, a state emergency is called. When there is a risk to the nation's ability to maintain its current level of financial wellbeing, the government will declare a state of economic catastrophe. Since a lockdown or stringent efforts to halt the outbreak of infection may harm the fundamental rights of citizens, it is necessary to investigate possible constitutional ways to incorporate health emergency in emergency legislation after conducting appropriate discussion with a variety of stakeholders.

3.3.2 COVID-19 Health Emergency: The Response of Union & the Concerns of State Govt.

For the first time in its history since gaining its independence, India was confronted with a significant challenge to its public safety and health in the form of the COVID-19. Legal experts have expressed worry over the Central Government's decision to impose a state-wide lockdown under DMA Sec. 6(2)(i), which was made without consulting them.[31] The announcement that was sent to all state govts. on March 24, 2020 by the Secretary of the Ministry of Home (MoH) ordered that all state & UT govts. give regular data on how the lockdown is being enforced in their respective jurisdictions. Ever since, the MoHFW[32] has put out rules about what precautions all state and UT governments need to take. There were some differing opinions about whether or not it was constitutional & lawful under DMA to order lockdown instructions.

The Hon'ble Prime Minister held teleconferences with the Chief Ministers of each state/UT govt. and other public officials to listen their ideas and concerns. The Central Govt made the decision to further extend already implement lockdown after conferring with the chief ministers of the states. The central government developed a number of fiscal stimulus programs, notably the "Pradhan Mantri Garib Kalyan Yojana," to boost the various government agencies.[33] There was still a lot of room for growth after the lockdown was lifted, even though stimulus spending was less than one percent of GDP. As per researcher's advice, the Central Govt must have worked largely on improving legal and constitutional measures so as to deal with a prospective medical emergency while leaving the Constitution's essential framework intact. This had been one of the shortcomings that was largely considered as a hindrance in coping with lockdown related challenges.

The requirement to improve local governments to cope up with a disease outbreak in aspects of checking, contact tracing, isolation beds, and accessibility of PPE was made worse by the growing number of instances and findings[34], as well as the fact that more information is available at the village level. In such a situation, more financial transfers to local governments were required which were found to be incompetent and less as compared to the required necessary demands which again made another set-back to government's approach. Finally, there were no mechanisms for resolving grievances in the act. With unusual and complex conditions, it was determined that people in this nation needed a structure for dealing with their problems at all levels of government. Therefore, lack of administrative and legislative imperatives was one of the main causes which lead to people being non-co-operative towards governmental strategies and their implementation.

Article 39 (e) of the constitution addresses the issue of workers' health protection. A unique situation, such as illness, disability, or old age is covered under Article 41 of the Constitution when public aid is provided by the state. Art. 42 protects both the health of the baby and the mother's health, so it is linked to maternity coverage in more than one way. Art. 47 asserts that it is the state's main job to promote public health, protect justice, make sure that workers have safe and fair working conditions, and provide more benefits for illness, impairment, old age, and childbirth. Also, the state has an obligation to limit the amount of alcohol people can drink for the good of the public as a whole. Art. 48A states that the state's job is to make sure that the environment is clean, safe, and healthy. On the other hand, these Directive Principles of State Policy can only be used to persuade people. Because they cannot be supported, it follows that a court of law would be unable to order that they be carried out. It is because of this that the state has used DPSP as a vehicle to get out of its duties and responsibilities to promote and maintain overall health in the people. In response, the apex court of India intervened and placed the right inside the purview of Art. 21. Everyone has the right to life and liberty, regardless of whether they are citizens or not, according to Art. 21. In the "Ram Lubhaya case"[35], the Court held that a person's right to health is associated with his or her responsibilities in the context of Art. 21, 41, as well as 47. As a consequence of the liberty granted by Art. 21, which is extended by Art. 47, the state is compelled to fulfil a comparable commitment. Even if the government has created a number of hospitals and schools, its job is not fulfilled until these institutions are available to the general public. In this judgement, it's worth remembering that the Supreme Court thought health was a holy, valuable, as well as sacrosanct right which should be kept safe. The Union and the States share legislative and executive authority under Indian Constitution, which is laid forth in the Seventh Schedule. It is possible that a number of items from the three categories are related to pandemics. The Union List, the State List, and the Concurrent List provide information on interstate movement, port quarantine, public health, and communicable diseases transfer from one state to another or even other states. Among other things, states are required to improve the third-tier administrations in the areas of healthcare and education after the 1992 73rd and 74th constitutional amendments (although this is not a mandatory requirement). As a result of this, the Municipal Commissioner has the authority to deal with the spread of pandemic illnesses, for example, through special State municipal regulations.[36] One may make the case that in dealing with COVID-19, all three levels of govt. have a major role. As a co-ordinating partner to the states, the federal govt. should only be accountable for interstate concerns, like port operations, and should not have the primary duty. States are responsible for public health and sanitation issues, such as planning and executing containment (monitoring and contact tracing, and quarantining) and mitigation plans. Anti-COVID-19 actions in most states are coordinated by the health secretary, a central government official. State-run hospitals and clinics provide the majority of healthcare services.[37] Due to the pandemic's impact on immigrant labour and the nation's finances, the concept of cooperative federalism was put to the test during the first lockdown. State control over an epidemic was largely restored during phase two of the shutdown when an acknowledgment of the sensitivities of states was made by central authorities

3.4 The Structure of Public Health Legislation

In general, public health is impacted by both direct and indirect laws. Ministry of health, agriculture, environmental protection and research and technology in India manage 67 of these statutes. The prevention and control of disease outbreaks necessitates laws that aren't tied to any particular danger or entrance point. Some of these are the "Births, Deaths, & Marriages Registration Act of 1886", "the Indian Red Cross Society Act of 1920", "the Drugs (Control) Act of 1950", and "the Consumer Protection Act of 1986".

Certain laws, on the other hand, are supervised by a number of different ministries. The "Drugs and Cosmetics Act (D&CA) of 1940", which is controlled by the "Ministries of Health and Family Welfare (MH&FW)", as well as "the Ministries of Chemicals and Fertilizers (MC&F)", is one of them. The D&CA of 1940, which is controlled by the MH&FW, as well as the MC&F, is one of them. Enforcing the "Environment (Protection) Act" of 1986 is the responsibility of the "Ministry of Environment & Forests (MR&F)", which works closely with the "Ministry of Science & Technology (MS&T)". The "Ministry of Food Processing (MFP)" and "the Ministry of Women and Children Development (MW&CD)" work together to carry out the "Feeding Bottles, Infant Milk Substitutes, & Infant Foods (Regulation of Production, Supply, and Distribution) Act", which was enacted in 1992. The "Department of Agriculture and Food" and the "Ministry of Agriculture and Rural Development" work together to run the "Destructive Insects and Pests Acts" of 1914 & 1992.

3.4.1 Epidemic Diseases Acts of 1897

There are only four sections to the act of 1897, making it a rather simple body of legislation. Specifically mentioned in the preamble was that the law's purpose was to prevent the spread of potentially lethal pandemic illnesses. It has gone into deeper depth on the relevance of the word dangerous when it comes to prefixing a pandemic with a disease. The Act pertains to the whole nation, although it delegated authority to the state governments for extraordinary actions and regulations, according to the Constitution. The authority for controlling dangerous pandemic diseases includes the prohibition of travel & social separation at points of entry, like airport & ports. The EDA of 1897 is in addition to, not in derogation of, the quarantine rule enshrined in the IPC of 1860. As a result, Sect. 3 & 4 of the EDA of 1897 are read in conjunction with Sec. 188, 269, 270, & 271 of the IPC of 1860 to achieve a comprehensive understanding of pandemic laws. Forty years after the EDA, 1897, was passed, the British colonial govt. finally realized the dire state of pandemic prevention. An Act of 1937 that authorized the Central Govt. to take steps and set regulations for inspecting any ship and detaining any person planning to sail/arrive at the port was the "Pandemic Diseases Amendment Act" of 1937. Sec. 2 & 2A[38] of the EDA, 1897, were invoked by the Central Govt. to enact social isolation, business closures, as well as travel bans in all Indian states & UTs to manage COVID-19. Those who violate quarantine & pandemic regulations will be punished under the EDA of 1897, Sec. 3, and Sec. 188 of the IPC of 1860. Similar to Sec. 133 of the "the Criminal Procedure Code of 1973", Sec. 4 of the Act excludes officials involved in pandemic prevention in good faith from criminal and civil penalties. The COVID-19 outbreak brought out the EDA of 1897 for the first time in 123 years.

A consequence of this is that any actions taken in response to an outbreak must take into account all relevant and significant problems.[39] The title of the act, as well as the extent of its implementation, are discussed in the first section. After that comes a discussion of state and national authorities' power to impose restrictions and take exceptional measures during deadly pandemics. Anyone can be given the authority to issue regulations or notices during a pandemic by the State Govt. in compliance with sec. 2 of the Act. While sec. 2A allows the Central Govt. the ability to enact protection and rules for vessel & ship examinations, and also to supervise anyone who plans to sail. Those who disobey public servant's orders are considered offenders under Sec. 188 of the IPC of 1860 and are subject to the penalties stipulated in the act, which are "six months' detention" and/or "a fine of Rs. 1000".[40] Sec.3 of EDA has been amended as a result of an order. Among the ministries involved in the direction and guidance, the MHF&W is particularly active. For its part, it provides other government departments with recommendations and newsletters, as well as announcing its findings. Several news conferences have been held by the MHF&W since 2019 to keep the public informed of developments in the country. Section 2 of the EDA, (amendment), 2020 mandates that state and territorial governments issue COVID-19 containment rules and notices to the public. After that, the rest of section talks about state-level legislative measures. It is customary for the elected administration to issue "a decree when the State Assembly is not in session"; however, this is not always the case. In the Odisha COVID19 Regulations of 2020 were adopted by the state govt. as the major act. The Epidemic Disease Act helped Telangana, a southern Indian state, adopt the "Pandemic Disease of Telangana (COVID-19) Regulation 2020." The State Director for Public Health, the Medical Education Director, and all district collectors, as well as the Police Commissioner and Police Superintendent, and all Municipal Corporation Commissioners, were all given the Power to administer and contain COVID19 under the provisions of the rule. The "State Integrated Surveillance Units", as well as the "District collector or commissioner of corporations", are mandated by state to receive all reports from all hospitals, governmental and non - governmental. Under the section 188 of "the Indian Penal Code, 1860", provides that those who refuse to comply with the Regulation may be prosecuted. In addition, the legislation outlaws the transmission of incorrect information in print media or on the social media, and those who violate the law may face legal penalties. Furthermore, the Telangana State Government has contributed to the preservation of robust and effective institutional institutions in order to keep COVID-19 at a minimum. Another South Indian state, utilising the Power granted by the EDA, issued the Karnataka Pandemic Outbreak, COVID-19 Regulations, 2020, under the auspices of the EDA. Private labs were not permitted to conduct COVID-19 testing under the terms of the regulations. For all specimens, the "District Nodal Officer" of the "Health and Family Welfare Department" of the relevant area must collect and deliver them to the authorized lab. In accordance with central guidelines, the specimens were collected. The act set up the "District Disaster Management Committee", which is led by "the Deputy Commissioner". Its key role is to make plans for dealing with disasters at the district level.[41] Similar to this, various state governments have adopted policies and strategic steps to oppose COVID-19 that are based on their respective institutional structures.

Before, the COVID-19 disease outbreak, some of the states had passed their own laws about public health or amended the EDA to encompass certain provisions. The Tamil Nadu Madras Public Health Act of 1939 is a comprehensive act on public health that was passed by the state legislature. It included the State Public Health Board, which comprised of a Minister for Public Health, additional Ministers for Coordination and Surgery, the Director of Health Services, a Health Engineer, and other State government candidates. This was established under the provisions of the Act, among other things. The "Madhya Pradesh Public Health Act" of 1949 is a similar legislative act in Madhya Pradesh. The Travancore-Cochin Public Health Act, 1955, for the southern and some portions of central Kerala, and the Madras Public Health Act, 1939, for the remainder of the State, are the two Acts that currently control the public health mechanism in the State of Kerala. [42]. In "the Himachal Pradesh Vaccination Act, 1968", the state government of Himachal Pradesh has already has a mandatory vaccination provision.

During breakouts, Bihar and Madhya Pradesh are the only two who have their own made state laws and administrations to apply during the notion. Since the EDA hasn't been fully put into place yet, it is up to each state govt. to make its own law and policies to deal with the same.

During the COVID-19 disease outbreak, several State govts. used the EDA to do what the Central Govt. told them to do. However, for pandemic containment in India, an integrated, comprehensive, responsive, and relevant legislative instrument is required. The EDA is currently insufficient for dealing with health crises such as COVID-19 because it lacks technological and operational capabilities for pandemic containment and management, as demonstrated by the COVID-19 outbreak.

When COVID-19 lockdowns, I, II, & III were implemented, the IPC, 1860, and Sec. 4 of the EDA, 1897, were exposed to public violence and harassment.[43] Due to this, the President of India used Art. 123 of the constitution to pass "the Pandemic Diseases (Amendment) Ordinance, 2020". This law came into force on 1st Jan. 2020. It has given the central govt. more power to control all kinds of mass transit, except for travel bans and violent acts, which the Ordinance has restricted (Sec. 2B). In Sec. 1Aa, there are definitions for aggressive acts. In Sec. 1Ab, there are definitions for healthcare & service workers, and also in Sec. 1Ab, there are definitions for medical institution property (Sec. 1Ac). "Acts of violence" have become a recognized and non-bailable crime that can get you between 3 months and 7 yrs. in jail and a penalty of Rs. 50,000 to Rs. 5 lakhs, regardless of the severity of the act. The Proposed law gives monetary compensation based on the market value or what the Court decides for healthcare service companies that get hurt or have their property damaged. First Information Report (FIR) analysis & trial are supposed to be completed by 30 days after the filing of the FIR, with a 6-months-extensible extension. The "Healthcare Personnel and Clinical Establishments (Prohibition of Violence, and Damage to Property) Bill, 2019[44]" and the "Pandemic Diseases (Amendment) Ordinance, 2020" work together to improve services.

On Apr. 22, 2020, "the Epidemic Diseases (Amendment) Ordinance, 2020" was enacted. The EDA of 1897 is amended by the Ordinance. The Act aims to stop the spread of epidemic illnesses that may be life-threatening. Protections for healthcare workers combating epidemic illnesses are included in the Ordinance, and the central government's authority to control their spread is augmented. The following are some of the Ordinance's most notable features: Legislation says that healthcare professionals are at risk of getting the pandemic outbreak while doing their work related to the disease. Those with the ability to stop the transmission of disease under the Act as well as those certified by the state authority are all covered in this group, as are public & medical professionals like doctors and nurses.

As an example, a healthcare worker may be subjected to any of the following acts of violence: Workers in the healthcare industry may be subjected to different types of abuse, including verbal or physical harassment, physical harm or danger to one's health or life, obstruction of one's job, or damage or loss to one's property or paperwork. An epidemic-related property is one in which a member of the healthcare industry has a direct stake. Examples of this kind of property include: clinics, wards, quarantine facilities, ambulances, and any other mobile medical units.

The Act gives the Central govt. the authority to check ships and other vessels that enter or leave ports and to hold people who try to leave ports during an epidemic. Even, they will now be able to check any vehicle or plane that leaves or arrives at a land port, port, or airfield. A person planning to travel by these methods may be detained at the discretion of the federal authorities. No one is allowed to: (i) harm a healthcare worker, or (ii) damage or destroy any property during an epidemic with the intent to harm or destroy healthcare workers or healthcare workers' property. Breaching this law is punishable with imprisonment for up to 5 months as well as a penalty from fifty to two lakh rupees. The victim may be allowed to file additional charges against this offender if the Court so orders. There is a maximum fine of five lakh rupees and up to seven years in prison for violence against healthcare professionals that leads to death or serious injury. They must be handled carefully because they are both cognizable & non-bailable. Under the Ordinance, those convicted of offences will also be required to pay the healthcare workers they injured compensation. The Court will decide how much money should be paid. If someone else's property is damaged or lost, the victim will get double the property's fair market value, as finally agreed by the Court. According to the "Revenue Recovery Act (RRA) of 1890," an arrear of land tax can be taken from any convicted person who fails to pay the fine. Police officers no lower than Inspector will examine any cases reported under the Ordinance. That date must be registered within thirty days of that time period. Within a year, the investigation or trial should be completed. As soon as this deadline has passed, the Judge must note the reason(s) for the delay and grant a further extension. There is a six-month limit on the length of the grace period. A person accused of inflicting serious injury to a member of the medical community will be presumed guilty of the crime until the opposite can be shown.

3.4.2 Disaster Management Act (DMA), 2005

When faced with an unprecedented public health disaster, the govt. has thoroughly examined the EDA of 1897's ability to tackle the COVID-19 outbreak. Art. 47[45] mandated it to promote public health, and it took it very seriously.[46] The COVID-19 outbreak has not been classified as a national disaster under Sec. 2(d) of the DMA of 2005 but as per Sec. 2(e) of the Act, the country lockdowns I (from 25th Mar, 2020 to 14th April, 2020), II (from 15th April, 2020 to 3rd May, 2020), as well as III (from 4th May, 2020 to 17th May, 2020) were necessary for central govt. disaster management. As part of its plan to be ready for a disaster that could be very bad, it adopted the capacity to deal with emergency prevention (Sect. 6), prevention (Sec. 7), preparedness (Sec. 8), as well as capacity building (Sec. 10) as coping skills. It took on the ability to cope capacity of emergency prevention and mitigation, or being ready, and building the capacity to handle situations or conditions that could lead to an emergency. The "National Disaster Management Authority (NDMA)" used its authority to modify all other rules and make sure that all Indian states followed it.

3.4.3 Essential Commodities Act (ECA), 1955

The worldwide pandemic's instability has taken its toll on health care systems, which have taken a heavy toll in recent times. While many may not be aware of it, India's recent second round of typhoons led to a significant scarcity of medical supplies, including oxygen cylinders and pulse meters. Even the government officials were tasked with ensuring that crucial supplies like masks and sanitizers, which were critical in the battle against the pandemic Covid-19, were not disrupted when the nation went into lockdown. Sanitizer and mask costs also went up at first because of the increased demand. Furthermore, a bad situation has been made worse by those who have hoarded necessities for the sake of profit and continue to do so. Essential Commodities Act, 1955, has been in force since 1955, and it was designed to deal with such situations (hereinafter referred to as "ECA").

As per Sec. 2A, for the objectives of governing the manufacture, supply, as well as distribution of basic goods, every item that is listed in the ECA's Schedule is considered to be eligible for consideration as an essential commodity.

The word "drugs" is the first thing on the ECA Schedule. It is an essential good. At this point, Sec. 3(b) of the "Drugs and Cosmetics Act of 1940" says that the focus should be on how certain advised medicines are defined and whether or not they are drugs. In 2020, Sec. 3(b) of the "Medications and Cosmetics Act, 1940" was changed by the "Ministry of Health and Family Welfare (MoHFW)" to encompass medical equipment as medicines. However, despite existing law, the government has been unable to address the significant shortcomings of the healthcare system due to its ageing - and nothing has been done to repair this.

It has been established that current regulations have inadequacies and that the central authority is unprepared to deal with an epidemic's second wave as a result. For example, the ECA rules that are currently in effect do not define "black marketing," and as a result, Section 7 of the ECA does not include any sanctions. Over 500 FIRs purportedly allege stockpiling and selling on the black market of oxygen cylinders, prescribed pharmaceuticals, and other commodities. This is without a doubt a big blunder in the legislative process.

According to the rules that are now in place, it is not considered illegal for a person to import medical equipment or to overcharge for medical drugs even if they do not possess the necessary licenses. Such with the over 500 oxygen concentrators that a Delhi resident imported and kept in his home, he cannot be held accountable for hoarding until the federal government notifies them under the ECA and sets a price for them.

As long as the channels used are authorized, the vendor is secure from any legal action. Even if it's unethical, the scenario isn't criminal. The stockpiling, adulteration, and black market selling of critical items has mostly harmed the lives of those with low incomes. A lack of oxygen tanks and the prohibitively expensive cost of medical supplies have resulted in the death of many individuals who otherwise might have survived.

As stated in Article 21 of the Indian Constitution, there have been grave abuses of the right to life and health. At the Supreme Court of India, a Public Interest Litigation (PIL) has been launched to expose our health infrastructure's failures, claiming our healthcare system is incapable of preventing hoarding, adulteration, and black sale of essential medical supplies. A public health crisis has been exacerbated by the government's inability to regulate the public health crisis due to regulations that are both ineffectual and out-of-date.

As a result of Venkateshwar Hospitals v. Govt. of NCT & Ors, the Hon'ble High Court of Delhi instructed the authorities to immediately notify the District Commissioner of any seizure or discovery of medical medicines or equipment. Because the scope of medical devices isn't clearly defined in ECA, authorities can't hold these criminals accountable under the present legislation for their actions. Even though in its order dated 25.04.2021, the Delhi Disaster Management Authority asserted the "Disaster Management Act," 2005, the "Epidemic Act 1897," and the "Indian Penal Code 1860" will punish those who engage in black marketing, adulteration, and hoarding, the definition of medical equipment has not been clarified, making the development insufficient.

In order to address the issue, it's not enough to merely amend Section 3 of the Drug and Cosmetic Acts, 1940 or the Essential Commodities Act. When it comes to the ECA, the central government has to make changes in order to address current and future problems effectively.

As a last point, it should be noted that the Constitution of India's Ninth Schedule has a particular mention for the Essential Commodities Act. Under the Art. 31B[47] which says that "no act, regulation, or provision that is said to be in conflict with or to limit any of the rights given by Part-III (Fundamental Rights) of the Constitution of India will be held to be invalid or to have become invalid." The main objective of the Commodities Act is to make sure that essential goods are made, sold, and distributed in a controlled way. The Schedule of the Act defines an essential commodity as a commodity that is listed in the Act.

3.4.4 The Public Health Bill

The National Public Health Bill[48], which has been in construction 2017 and later in 2022, would substitute the Epidemic Diseases Act, 1897, which has been in effect for 125 years. The draught Bill suggests granting state and municipal governments the power to effectively respond in a range of circumstances to public health emergencies like epidemics and bioterrorism. This Bill was created by the National Center for Disease Control and the Directorate General of Health Services. In these provisions regarding monitoring of public health emergencies, disease notification, disasters, and bioterrorism will be updated comprehensively as well as scientifically.

As per section 2, "the terms 'epidemic', 'isolation', 'quarantine', and 'social distancing' all defined in the Bill as well as specific definitions for 'public health emergency of international concern', 'ground crossing', 'disinfection', 'deratting', and 'decontamination' have been provided".

As per section 3, it has given states and local governments the authority to take the necessary actions - such as placing people in quarantine, cleaning up areas, isolating infectious agents and performing spot checks in the circumstance of a public health emergency. A four-tiered system of health administration is anticipated in the new bill, with national, state, district, and local public health officials, each with distinct roles and duties for handling public health emergencies. In the first-tier state health ministers would serve as members of the national public health authority. It will headed by the Union Health Ministry. District Collectors would be in charge of the second tier, and at the further tier Block Medical Officers or Medical Superintendents would be in charge. These authorities will have the power to combat new infectious diseases and non-communicable diseases with preventive measures. It also enables state and union territory authority to undertake any medical examinations including laboratory tests as well as to administer vaccinations or other treatments for any diseases to individuals who have been exposed to them or who are ill or are suspected of being ill with them.

The relevance of the concerned person's authorization for carrying out such medical or laboratory examinations, as well as for administering vaccinations or treatments, is not addressed by the clause.

It incorporates three distinct elements—epidemics, disasters, and bioterrorism—each of which has a unique scope and cannot be pigeonholed into a single paradigm for response. In contrast to an epidemic or disaster the response strategy for bioterrorism will be very different and consequently, the duties and responsibilities of various governmental organisations and agencies will alter. Additionally, it would be crucial to establish complementarity and prevent conflict among the sections of the possible Public Health Act because many of them would end up overlapping with those of the Disaster Management Act, 2005. Although the Epidemic Act has been renamed the Public Health Act, the major focus will probably still be on epidemics. This would imply that it lives up to its name, yet being extremely wide in breadth is neither sensible nor prudent. It's crucial to know where to draw the line, and while the new Bill should keep public health emergencies as its main priority, it should also always recognize the holistic character of emergency responses and widen its focus to include other closely linked issues.

3.5 Overall Data and Analysis of Response of India to Pandemic in Three Stages

Some of the world's most advanced healthcare systems were shattered by the epidemic. In order to determine the degree of COVID-19 spread in any nation, screening was determined to be important. Coronavirus infections may have gone undetected in India because of the country's low testing ratio. India lags behind with a rate of approximately ten tests per million individuals[49]. Prior to the nationwide lockdown, the govt's testing methodology was based on the assumption that there was no community spread in India and that all instances had been imported from elsewhere. This presumption has been proven false.

The testing technique had unforeseen repercussions for the spread of the pandemic since it was based on these assumptions, as well as the fact that it only tested those who had travelled from contaminated regions abroad. The lockdown did indeed cause a huge number of employees to relocate domestically from established hotspots such as Mumbai and Delhi to their home states, hence increasing the overall spread of illness throughout the whole country. Inability to recognize the occurrence of Covid-19 infectious diseases in the community and to test all people with symptoms, especially in areas of Mumbai as well as Delhi with the highest percentage of disease infections, led to the disease spreading in all these states and a possible eruption of case scenarios in regions with less established healthcare system. This resulted in some discriminatory tactics being implemented against select states and localities with a high prevalence of infection to contain the transmission of the disease. As a result, the disease was able to be contained. At the outset of its national shutdown, it was discovered that India lacked sufficient testing kits, despite the fact that the government had issued licenses to private businesses to sell them in India. The quantity of laboratories available for testing also proved to be a limitation. On March 23, 2021 neither Arunachal Pradesh (with 1.5 million people) nor Nagaland (with 3.3 million people) had any testing clinics. Bihar, with 110 million people, had only one approved lab, whereas Rajasthan, with 80 million people, had 8. There were also vast geographical differences; neither Arunachal Pradesh nor Nagaland had testing facilities. Despite how many test kits were sent to states, govt. labs were unable to utilize them since their daily testing capacity was limited to ninety specimens. Due to the findings of these tests, the govt. has authorised private companies -to do COVID-19 testing, allowing those who are not hospitalised to be tested, albeit at their own expense. In India, the govt's price cap of Rs. 4500 (around 55 euros) per test was prohibitively expensive for the great majority of individuals, particularly if the cap was expanded to cover family testing. Due to the high cost of private testing and the logistical complications of the lockout, the vast number of Indians were anticipated to rely solely on the public test procedure. The public healthcare system in India is already overworked and underfunded, and spending money on coronavirus testing reduces funding for other public health concerns.

In 2021, the nation only spent 3.7 percent of its financial plan on healthcare. There was an insufficient funding to address the tremendous need for critical care in nations that had already been hit by Covid-19, and the budget was simply too modest. It was projected that approximately 5 percent of patients in India who were contaminated with Covid-19 necessary critical care, and also that half of those who were hospitalised to an ICU required mechanical ventilation. At the peak of the pandemic, there was a demand for up to one million ventilators. Statistics provided by the Ministry of Health indicated that there were 8432 ventilators in government hospitals; however, if private institutions were included in the calculation, the total number of ventilators may reach 50,000. To put this into perspective, during the 2009 COVID-19 epidemic in the US, the nation only had 164,000 ventilators available for a populace that was just 1/3rd the size of India's. Its domestic production capability was 5000 ventilators per month, and it has reliant on outside suppliers for a few necessary elements, like the fan motor. Thus, India has imported approximately 75 percent of the ventilators it has manufactured. As a result of Public Health Service challenges and the incidence of unaffordable private healthcare in several Indian states, the Covid-19 response to the crisis should have prioritised bolstering an accessible and affordable healthcare system for all citizens, whether they are wealthy/poor, Hindu/Muslim or from Bihar/Kerala. But the pandemic showed that the vast large percentage of Indians are incredibly and horribly vulnerable to a tragedy which goes far beyond healthcare. Also, and this is very different from the risk of getting sick, the lockdown used to contain contagious diseases has made a lot of people's lives worse because of how the virus affects the body.[50] In accordance with Art. 21 of Indian Constitution, it was ultimately determined that the pandemic violated our fundamental rights.[51]

3.6 Case Studies

(1) Re: Cognizance for extension for limitation[52]

Judges: CJI N.V. Ramanna, J. L. Nageshwar Rao and J. Surya Kant.

Facts of the Case

Covid-19, a deadly pandemic affected the entire judicial system along with the administrative constitution of all nations, their economy and medical health infrastructure. Only the urgent cases and matters were allowed to be heard through video conferencing. The Hon'ble Supreme Court took Suo Moto notice in March 2020 taking in account the difficulty being faced by litigants they were facing while submitting petitions, applications, suits, appeals. Further, it ordered an extension of the statute of limitation until further orders.

Due to the return of normalcy and the decline in the prevalence of the Covid-19 virus, the Hon'ble Supreme Court determined on March 8, 2021, to withdraw the extension of limitation from March 14, 2021. On the request of the Supreme Court Advocate on Record Association, the Hon'ble Court issued an order on April 27, 2021, restoring the extension of the limitation period until further orders.

The Election Commission of India made a request for modification of the judgement extending the limits on election petitions in September 2021 because of worries about the challenge of keeping Electronic Voting Machine and election papers forever.

Issue of the Case

Litigants suffer numerous problems in filing petitions, suits and appeals in the court due to limitation period prescribed by the law.

Held

The hon'ble court had given order extending the limitation period from 15th march, 2020 until further orders. On 6 may, 2020, it was held that the period of 15 days shall be given to all the litigants after the lockdown period finishes. The Hon'ble Supreme Court of India exercised its powers as conferred to it under article 142 read along with article 141.

On 23 September 2021, the Apex Court rescinded the extension of the time restriction, effective October 2, 2021, despite of the fact that the Supreme Court asked to recall order which was contingent onto the third wave of the Covid-19 pandemic's uncertainty, the order was reinstated. Following a surge in Covid-19 instances, the Hon'ble Supreme Court of India reinstated the limitation extension in January 2022. The Apex Court's judgement of 10 January 2022 excused the time from 15 March 2020 to 28 February 2022 for the purposes of limitation.

Effects of the Case

This order had an overriding effect on all legal regulations. It was a binding order which applied to all the acts including arbitration and conciliation and Negotiable Instrument Act, 1881. When the Supreme Court issued its first judgement to extend the limitation time, the Delhi High Court noted that the lockdown period would not be incorporated in the law of limitation until additional rulings were made. These orders were made to do complete justice to the citizens of this nation.

Conclusion

This was one of the best decisions taken by the Apex court which did justice to the litigants as well as the citizens. The Hon'ble Supreme Court of India showed its wits acting within the time hence, taking into account that as it was held in **Hussainara Khatoon Case**[53],

Speedy Justice is the heart of fundamental value of justice. Due to online proceedings, technical errors due to adoption of new system with respect to virtual proceedings, quarantine lockdown and wide spread of Corona virus disease, accessibility of public was getting reduced. Advocates were not able to convey notices in time. Emails and communication gaps were witnessed. Therefore, court appropriately realized that it would be unfair to consider the case being barred by lapse of time as it was act of calamity and God wherein entire nation was facing hardship. In the light of prevailing circumstances courts took substantial realties on record and rightly dismissed the consideration of limitation period for the duration India was facing Pandemic.

(2) Re: Distribution of Essential Supplies and Services during pandemic[54]

Judges: J. Dr. D.Y. Chandrachud, J. L. Nageshwar Rao and J. Ravindra Bhatt

Facts of the Case

The second wave of the worldwide COVID-19 pandemic, which has been deadlier and much more terrifying around the globe, particularly in India, had arrived. The number of cases were increasing day by day and people making people suffer more. The number of available hospital beds and oxygen was found to be rapidly diminishing. Essential drugs were low in their supply and scarcity of medicines was increasing leading to increased deaths along with worst condition of patients. Due to these conditions, the hon'ble Supreme Court took up suo moto cognizance, to make certain that the people of India are provided with critical services and commodities throughout the pandemic.

A well pronounced judgement was delivered by the Supreme Court of India addressed, various issues among other things such as vaccination policies, the provision of medicine and oxygen to healthcare facilities and healthcare workers, and concerns about freedom of speech and expression during the COVID1-9 pandemic.

The order inculcated the directions to the Central and State/ UT governments regarding the management of vaccination drives, supply of essential drugs and identifying vulnerable age groups in accordance with the changing nature of pandemic.

The Supreme Court appointed eminent Advocates named as Jaideep Gupta and Meenakashi Arora as amicus curae. This case was all about issues faced by the general public of India during second wave of deadly pandemic. Oxygen demand and the efforts took to ensure its supply were discussed in the present case. Allocating oxygen to states and UTs and communicating often about the need was primary focus of court. The number of unoccupied beds at medical facilities became a serious concern. Court realized the important of steps that might be taken to ensure the availability of vital pharmaceuticals and also regulated their pricing along with taking strict note of the fact that practices such as stockpiling are controlled. Measures being taken to get the second dosage of vaccinations, as well as the amount of vaccines that will be required were taken into account. How vaccinations were being allocated to states and why vaccines were sold overpriced was the important question that the Hon'ble Court faced. The said judgement took cognizance of all the above said points and aspects with respect to healthcare and dealt with them.

Then Solicitor General emphasized with respect to the distribution of vaccination that the whole country will be immunized by the end of 2021, and that the Central Government is working with several international entities to secure vaccine supplies.

Special Leave Petition was reviewed by the Supreme Court of India in response to a High Court of Delhi judgement involving the supply of medical oxygen to the National Capital Territory of Delhi. In order to successfully combat a disease, health experts throughout the globe thought that immunising the whole eligible population of a country is the sole most important task. The vaccination issue was significant in the said regard.

Policies Regarding Vaccination

From January 16 to February 2, healthcare staff and frontline workers were vaccinated as part of the first phase. At the beginning of the second phase in 2021, adults over 60 years of age and 45 years of age with specific co-morbidities, and all people over 45 years of age, were eligible to get the vaccine.

There should be a 50/50 split between vaccine makers supplying to the federal government and states/UTs and private hospitals procuring the remainder. The cost of vaccinations at private hospitals will be monitored. A free vaccination programme for eligible individuals will be offered to those who obtain their doses from the UOI. The Union of India has been asked to explain the parameters of vaccine procurement and distribution in the coming months. In addition, UoI was tasked with providing information on the anticipated number of vaccinations and the manufacturing efforts required to meet that goal.

The Central Government has established the projected eligible population of each state, and states are only allowed to purchase vaccinations for that population. Every two weeks, the Center will provide updated information on the total number of distributions made to each state.

As part of the new Liberalized Vaccination Policy, the total number of vaccinations manufactured will be split 50:25:25 between the federal government, state and local governments, and private institutions. Without strict regulation, the dosages may be offered to patients at private hospitals at substantially higher costs. In order to negotiate a better bargain for other private organisations, they may not sell all vaccinations via CoWIN. Because these facilities are located in major metropolitan centres, fewer vaccinations will be available in rural regions.

Differential Pricing Effects

Difference in pricing was implemented to encourage competition and to bring in more vaccine makers to enable quick immunisation, according to an affidavit filed by the UoI on May 9, 2021. For States/ UTs and private health care facilities to purchase vaccinations, producers must disclose the price in an easy-to-understand manner. Vaccinations will be provided free of charge to everyone, regardless of age.

Since free vaccination has been guaranteed by the States/UTs, the Central Government said that the ultimate conclusion will be unaffected by the Liberalized Vaccination Policy. However, the Union of India is urged to use its position as a monopoly buyer in the market to pass on the benefits to all citizens.

Diversification as the Foundation for Price Division

Covishield and Covaxin vaccinations were the focus of the UoI's efforts to reduce prices and improve quality.

Issues

The hon'ble Supreme Court dealt with number of issues regarding following:

1. the supply of oxygen
2. The supply of essential drugs that has to be provided for the citizens who is in need.
3. Giving directions to the central or state/UT governments regarding the management of vaccination drives.
4. Effects of differential pricing and providing all the necessary information regarding vaccination.

Observations

Health care providers, front-line workers, and those over the age of 45 were given priority in receiving the COVID-19 vaccinations, according to the Supreme Court of India. There are a number of people who will have to pay for vaccinations under the Liberalized Vaccination Policy. An illness that has caused significant health problems, including hospitalisation and even death, has been reported in people aged 18 to 44.

Increased vaccine production and availability is another concern raised by the Supreme Court. Because vaccine demand is reliant on a variety of circumstances, including the introduction of new vaccines from other countries and the capacity of current producers to boost production, the Supreme Court of India has taken notice of Union of India's arguments in its affidavit.

When asked if vaccination costs damage the poor and disadvantaged, India's Apex Court noted that every State/UT has pledged to vaccinate its inhabitants free of charge, according to its affidavit, which was included in the Central Government's answer.

The Honorable Supreme Court of India also noted that the Liberalized Vaccination Policy had resulted in a split in responsibility for vaccination in phase 3 between the federal government and state/UT governments and private institutions (for people over 45, healthcare workers and frontline workers) (for the age group of 18-44 years). State and federal governments will have to work together to share the limited vaccine logistics in the State/UT. Instead, the federal government purchases and distributes vaccines to states and territories as part of the Universal Immunization Program, ensuring that their cold storage facilities are not overloaded.

In the case of Jacobson v. Massachusetts, 197 U.S. 11 (1905), the Supreme Court of the United States examined a constitutional liberty challenge to a smallpox vaccination law. The Hon'ble Supreme Court of India acknowledges the dynamic character of the measures in light of the current public health crisis in India. As the pandemic spreads, governments throughout the world have been given additional leeway to implement regulations that would have previously infringed on individual liberties but are now vital to fight the pandemic.

Held

All issues and concerns raised must be addressed in an affidavit submitted to the Honorable Supreme Court of India by the Union of India, so that no matter is left unanswered. The Hon'ble apex court also ordered Union of India to attach to its affidavit copies of all relevant documents and file notes outlining its thoughts and culminating in the vaccination policy. Affidavits from the Union of India must be submitted within two weeks. The apex court instructed the state and UT administrations to confirm or deny the viewpoint. To ensure that the citizens of their jurisdiction may get free vaccines at a state vaccination centre, they must include this policy in their affidavit as a matter of principle in their application. Because of this, the Supreme Court of India has issued a two-week deadline for each state/UT administration to submit a written document explaining its stance and outlining its specific policies.

Conclusion/Comment

Court had directed the UOI for some measures regarding the supplies and providing services regarding essential things for all the citizens of the country during this horrifying period. U.O.I. was required to provide information on the quantity of vaccinations administered, including information on the first and second doses, the vaccination schedule for the remainder of the population, and the central government's full purchase data for all COVID-19 vaccines. The hon'ble Supreme Court has been obliged to do complete justice as it is the foremost duty. Judges themselves being victimized of covid and deaths caused due to the same on humanitarian grounds knew how important accessibility of vaccination is and hence,

for accessibility the black marketing of vaccines going on wherein money was being given greater priority than human life violated the principles of humanity. Hence, court had to interfere so that state and center could regulate the ill practices going on in market in the name of medical facilities.

(3) Re: Contagion of Covid 19 Virus in Prisons[55]

Judges: CJI, J. L. Nageshwar Rao and J. Surya Kant

Facts of the Case

On March 16, 2020, the honourable Supreme Court of India took suo moto notice of overcrowding of jails throughout the country and observed that it is not simple for jail prisoners to maintain social separation in order to prevent the spread of coronavirus. The number of people infected with COVID-19 is "historically rising" throughout the nation. In jails across the globe, overcrowding has become a major concern. As people does not have open environment and are leaving in a common place. Contagious illnesses may spread more quickly if inmates aren't kept apart due to overcrowding.

India's Supreme Court ruled on May 7, 2021, to provide some respite to jailed convicts in the country's prisons. A number of high-powered committees were formed on March 23, 2020, and their recommendations led to the release of many inmates, either on bond or parole, at that time.

After a significant reduction in the number of ongoing cases, inmates are sent back to jail. Nearly 400,000 inmates remain behind bars in India, with the majority of them returning to their cells after the issuance of release orders. As a result of COVID-19, inmates who were released on parole as a result of their convictions have been required to post an interim bond of at least 90 days.

On parole, those who have served less than seven years in jail will be allowed to leave the facility. As a result of Arnesh Kumar v. State of Bihar (2014), which said that arrests should be an exception in situations where the offences are punished by less than seven years of imprisonment, the Supreme Court has decided that the police would not undertake arrests.

The Apex Court have given directions to the central or state government to constitute a high-powered committee for taking decisions related to prisoner's interim bail or parole. Court's concern towards prison inmates who don't want to get released because of social status and fear of contracting COVID-19.

Issues

1. According to a statement released by the WHO and other international agencies, the COVID-19 epidemic has made convicts more vulnerable. However, prisoners in jails as well as correctional facilities suffer significant risk due to the isolation and close quarters they share with their fellow prisoners.
2. Due to overpopulation in Indian prisons, the government requested that inmates who refuse to be released be provided with basic medical care.
3. Need for prison-based pandemic management in order to battle this lethal virus."
4. Authorities should not be allowed to arrest persons who do not meet the requirements specified by this court, the judge said.
5. Because of this, the risk of infection and dissemination of COVID-19 in many jail systems needed to be significantly increased.
6. Keeping the convicts in a clean and safe environment was the most demanding responsibility.
7. There were serious problems for women incarcerated as the COVID-19 outbreak continues to cause havoc on prisons.
8. As a result of their regular interaction with criminals, law enforcement and healthcare professionals working in prisons were suffering from higher risk of contracting infectious diseases.
9. Women in prison were more likely to be sexually assaulted and to contract diseases transmitted by others because they lacked equal access to gender-sensitive basic healthcare, proper nutrition, and protection from violence.

Observations

Overcrowding in prison is a concerned matter and court consider and made various directions to the central or state government. The Apex Court had directed them to form high powered committees so that the work of choosing prisoners on the basis of their performance were delegated. The court had made guidelines for jail decluttering in the midst of COVID-19 made several changes with respect to prisoners. In addition, the Court has declared that detainees are more susceptible to the spread of infectious diseases in prisons. Article 21 of India's Constitution guarantees all citizens a fundamental right: to live. As a result, it is necessary to decongest and improve jail conditions so that all government measures can be made available to all citizens at large, in accordance with Article 21 of the Indian Constitution.

Judgement

The Hon'ble apex court in its judgement considered that the monotony of the prison environment may be exacerbated by a lack of connection with family members. Drug use and sex between same-sex couples are encouraged in this setting. To prevent boredom, some individuals participate in these types of activities. There is a serious public health threat if dangerous lifestyles go uncontrolled, resulting in disease transmission from one prisoner to another. It is not part of a prisoner's punishment to become sick while in custody. For deadly diseases, such as COVID-19 or HIV/AIDS this consideration becomes even more critical.

In order to prevent the deadly virus from spreading among convicts, it is critical that daily hygiene and sanitation standards be maintained and necessary measures be implemented. Many jails are too full, and because of this, inmates have been overlooked for a long time. Because of this, they don't have the basic infrastructure, equipment, and people needed to take basic steps to stop and control a health disease outbreak. Indian courts have instructed all states to examine releasing certain inmates on parole to reduce prison overcrowding, as well as a "High-Powered Committee" to rule on the matter. Early parole eligibility for offenders serving sentences of below 7 yrs. was mandated by the SC in order to relieve prison overcrowding. Arrests should only be made as an exception in situations where the maximum sentence is below 7 yrs. in jail, according to the SC ruling in Arnesh Kumar v. State of Bihar (2014).

As a sentinel on the qui vive (a watchful protector) of Final Report, this Court must strictly limit as well as restrict the officials from holding a suspect in a way that goes against the standards set out in "Arnesh Kumar v. State of Bihar" during the outbreak. According to the CJI, a High-Level Committee in partnership with the Legal Service Authority of the State should be formed to determine whether or not convicted criminals can be released on parole or interim bail for an amount of time that is considered acceptable. Additionally, the HPC might select whether inmates should be freed based on the kind of crime they committed, the length of time they have served, the gravity of the charges they are facing, or any other relevant consideration. This directive also urged the high-powered committees to implement the National Legal Services Authority's guidelines on the release of new detainees as part of their consideration. Additionally, the HPC, comprised of "the State Legal Services Committee Chairman", "the Principal Secretary (Home/Prison)" by whatever name they go by, and the Director-General of Jail, is tasked with determining which inmates are eligible for parole or interim bail for whatever time period is deemed appropriate. The High-Powered Committee, Delhi, also indicated that Delhi's Commissioner of Police will be a member of the committee.

Directions/Held

Directions given by the court will be applicable on all the offences that are punishable with imprisonment for a term that is seven years or less than that. On or after May 23, 2020, those who were released under an order should be given another 90 days of parole and those who were released on probation should be given another 90 days of probation. High Powered Committees' judgments and the number of inmates in jail need to be posted on the relevant websites. The concern of those prisoners who don't want to get released because of their social status and dread of getting covid 19 needs to be consider.

A warrant must be obtained before a police officer may arrest a suspect under section 498A of the Indian Penal Code, which prohibits an immediate arrest. Before approving detention, the magistrate must note his or her satisfaction with the accused's appearance before him or her. Even if the officer decides not to make an arrest, the magistrate must be notified. Section 41A of the CrPC mandates that a notice of appearance be issued on the accused within two weeks of the date of the arrest. The Magistrate and the authorities who fail to comply with these orders face departmental action and contempt of court charges before the appropriate High Court.

Conclusion/Comment

The Courts since years' work on the principle of that even if thousands of criminals remain unpunished, a single innocent must not get punished. Delayed trials when a person is only accused and not proven to be guilty is not less than being punished for nothing because you are suffering in prison with a status quo of an accused. Apart from that, pathetic conditions of jails were leading to inmates suffer from corona and delayed trials were acting as a hindrance to the rule of equity, justice and good conscience. Therefore, the courts rightly issued favourable guidelines taking in account that even people accused of crime have their own rights which are to be protected.

(4) Ficus Pax Private Ltd. & Ors. v. Union of India & Ors.[56]

Judges- J. Ashok Bhushan, J. Sanjay Kishan Kaul and J. M Shah

Facts of the Case

Working people were facing various consequences because of covid 19 outbreak. Many people lost their jobs and some didn't get their salary for surviving in the inflated environment. According to a Ministry of Labor and Employment advisory of March 20th, 2020, businesses should not terminate or reduce the pay of employees who were on leave. The Ministry of Home Affairs (MHA) then published a directive on March 29th, 2020, instructing companies to pay their employees' wages on time even if they were unemployed or had little money. The Hon'ble Supreme Court of India received a number of petitions contesting the circular issued by the MHA and the Ministry of Labor and Employment after it was released.

In these petitions, it was argued that the circular issued infringed the constitutional rights of employers guaranteed by Article 14 and Article 19(1)(g). The petitioner also included the following points:

1. The ESIC (Employee's State Insurance Corporation), PM-CARES (The Prime Minister's Citizen Assistance and Relief

in Emergency Situations Fund), or any other Government funds/ schemes, can pay 70% to 80% of the salary during the lockdown time.

2. ESI and the Provident Fund will be eliminated.
3. Permission to pay half of the base salary and the dearness allowance in one lump sum.
4. Enforcement of the state circular quashing orders made by several State Governments.
5. Employer/worker failure to pay wages necessitates intervention by the government.

On 2nd June, 2020, the then Attorney General of India, informed the Hon'ble Supreme Court that the Circular released was not simply for migrant workers, but that the primary goal of said circular was to ensure that employees would not need to move if they were compensated. The decision was important since there were more then 150 million migrant workers, and if they are unable to meet their basic needs, they will return to their homes in other states and towns, where they may spread the illness because they will have to travel for miles to get there.

As a result of many mediation requests made by the employees' union in support of the circular, the court permitted them to be combined with the case of Ficus Pax Private Limited v. Union of India and Others and all of the related petitions. As of the 18th of May 2020, all orders made by authorities under Section 10(2) (1) of the Disaster Management Act will cease to be in force due to the petitioners, i.e. the employers, being granted temporary relief by the Supreme Court on the 15th of May 2020. As a response to many complaints, Union of India filed a counter Affidavit on June 4, 2020, stating the legal authority under which the circular was passed and the events and circumstances surrounding its withdrawal.

Issues raised by Union of India

According to the Labors Act and the Indian Constitution's Articles 14 and 21, workers in India have forgone their right to salaries. Disaster Management Act Section 10(1) gives the authority to issue this Circular. The MHA circular is reasonable and consistent, and it serves the public interest. In order to alleviate the financial burden on workers, the company has issued a circular. Inability to pay workers' salaries is not a valid justification to question the authority of legislative authorities, according to the argument.

Issues Raised by Employers

In these petitions, it was argued that the circular issued infringed the constitutional rights of employers guaranteed by Article 14 and Article 19(1)(g). By having to pay the employees, the steady firm would go bankrupt since it will have no source of revenue to pay the workers out of. This act is in direct violation of articles 14 and 19 (1) (g) of our constitution, even though the private sector is able to impose financial obligation on the government.

Held/Observed

The hon'ble Supreme Court gave its interim order on 12th June, 2020. According to the petitioner's argument, Articles 14 and 19 (1) (g) of the Constitution do not permit imposing financial burden on workers, hence any obligation imposed on employers during the 50-day period must be ruled out since it is contrary to the Articles' stated intent.

Everyone agreed that the lockdown had an equal impact on employees and companies alike, and that each industry has its own unique working and financial capacities, so not all firms would go bankrupt as a result of having to pay employees' salaries.

In light of this, businesses and employees must strike a fair balance when it comes to resolving the wage dispute that has been raging for the past 50 days despite the fact that employees want to work for them but are unable to do so because of the country's lockdown.

Additionally, the Court ruled that the settlement should not affect the rights of employers and employees that are now being litigated through writ petitions in front of the Court, and it also instructed that the workers be permitted to work notwithstanding the continuing wage-arrears issue between them.

A temporary injunction was issued by the court to discuss and collect the arrears of salaries for all businesses that were either shut down or only functioning at a reduced capacity for 50 days during that time period.

Conclusion

Nation is still suffering with the shattered economy and other impact of Covid 19 wherein GDP is degenerating day by day and many people lost their employment due to companies getting into loss and winding up. Hence, looking at the condition of employees who were working without any hope of payment, Hon'ble Court rightly issued the directions in favour of daily wagers, employees and labours along with their employers to maintain the economic balance as far as was feasible. Neither employers could be compelled to stretch their pockets beyond limit nor the employees could be expected to survive in mascarre and hence, government support and intervention was necessary.

(5) Ramakrishna S/o Rangaiah v. The U.O.I. and Ors.[57]

Judges- J. D.V.S.S.Somayajulu, Lalitha Kanneganti

Facts of the Case

During the lockdown period, a large number of daily wage workers lost their work and were not able to earn for their livelihood. They started returning back to their ancestral homes or hometowns in search of some food to eat or place to live. People who were migrate to big cities for better livelihood were now forced to return back. Migrant workers with their children and luggage are trekking along the National Highways in the sweltering summer heat, notably in the state of Andhra Pradesh. Petition under Section 151 CPC requested that the High Court may be pleased to direct the Respondents to immediately provide the Migrant Workers stranded in Vijayawada, Guntur, and other parts of the State of Andhra Pradesh, due to the extension of the National Lockdown declared in the State of Andhra Pradesh, to receive necessary essential food material, immediate financial aid in cash, and safe accommodation.

The petitioner prayed that these people work for us day and night. Now they need us. We have to reduce their pain or sufferings. All articles or survey had been submitted clearly showed how poor migrant workers were migrating continuously. According to reports in a famous English newspaper, a woman hasd given birth while travelling from Nasik to Sathani on the roadside. According to the study, a woman began walking two hours after giving birth and went on to walk for 150 kilometres.

Observation/Held

The Court was well aware of the fact that the labour who had left their ancestral homes and villages in search of a better life for themselves and their families were on the highways today. A wide range of occupations and callings were represented by them. The court realized that it was their duty to protect them during the said crisis and reduce their pain and sufferings. Andhra Pradesh's summer heat was intensifying and the Court had noticed that hundreds of migrants with their children and luggage were still wandering on the National Highways despite the summer. According to reports, food counters had been set up at a distance of 50 kilometres from each other in order to aid the migrating population. Relief centres had been built as well.

Judgement

The Hon'ble HC of Andhra Pradesh stated and observed that:

"This Court is aware that there are people working today who have left their ancestral towns and villages and moved to the city in the hope of providing a better life for themselves and their family. These people can be found on the roadways.

Together, they represent a wide range of occupations and professions, which all contribute to our well-being in a variety of ways. Now, if this court does not act to safeguard the people and alleviate their suffering, it will be failing in its responsibility. Efforts must be made to ease their discomfort at this point. Article 21 of the Indian Constitution's ever-expanding definition of "lite" will take this scenario into consideration. The fact that they are walking back with their heads held high instead of living at someone's mercy shows that they deserve additional assistance. This order is in continuation of the preceding order dated 23.04.2020 and is made with that goal in mind. The counter-affidavit submitted and the representations made show that the State Govt., in accordance with the Central Govt. orders, provides considerable assistance to migrant workers and labourers who are on the move. The government also provides some more information. This Court, notwithstanding the efforts of the federal and state governments, believes that more must be done. We've also read a few troubling articles in the newspaper. Estimates from "Eenadu" reveal that 1300 individuals went through a single checkpoint on foot or by bicycle in a 24-hour period between 13.05.2020 and 14.05.2020. Another 1,000 people were transported by lorry or other means of transportation. According to accounts in a well-known English publication, a lady gave birth while travelling the route between Nasik and Sathani. In addition, one article states that the mother began walking two hours after giving birth and walked for 150 kilometres. The "National Commission on Human Rights" is aware of this issue, which was brought to their attention. According to the reports, even for relatively short distances, ambulance services in Mumbai might cost as much as Rs. 8,000/-. Because of how grave the current state of affairs is, this Court feels compelled to step in and take action right now. Despite the rising temperatures, especially in the state of Andhra Pradesh, this Court has seen hundreds of migrant workers travelling the National Highways with their children and luggage. It has been reported that food stations have been set up at a distance of every 50 kilometres for the benefit of migrants. The establishment of relief centres is also mentioned. However, in light of the aforementioned, the following additional actions should be implemented immediately and on a priority basis:"

Health and Well-being

Because of the extreme heat, the so-called state-established outposts or tents should not be just takeout counters but instead should be equipped with appropriate supplies of decent drinking water, oral dehydration salts, and glucose packets that should be provided to the migrant labourers travelling. Sunstroke victims should have access to trained paramedics and/or a doctor on call, as well as a cell phone and an ambulance on standby, at every centre. The state should provide ambulances on call to transport migrant workers to the closest hospitals or medical facilities where they may get prompt medical attention at no expense to the worker.

Change Rooms and Toiletries

Because so many women are out in the heat, sanitary restrooms and other public conveniences should be made available to ensure the women's privacy. Ideally, there should be dispensing devices for sanitary pads in every alternate centre.

Culinary Delicacies

Provisions for meals should be created and supplied to migrant workers crossing the Nation Highway on foot. There are a great number of volunteers who are feeding these migrants, but they are doing it on a one-on-one basis. Numerous wealthy industrialists, companies, and corporations are launching their own efforts, as well. As part of their CSR activities, corporations and other organisations can assist the state government give free meals to these migrants. In order to ensure that the prepared food is delivered to the migrant workers who are on the road, all interested members of the public, non-profit organisations, and other groups should coordinate their efforts.

Patrol cars operated by the Indian National Highways Authority and the Indian Police Force are always on the road. Any migrant workers who are having problems getting to a shelter on their own should be picked up and transported using these vehicles. And this is in addition to the state buses already in operation.

There are five types of pamphlets

As migrant workers go along the highways, they should be given brochures in Hindi and Telugu that tell them where their shelters are and what phone numbers they may call in an emergency.

Measures to ensure safety include

In order to maintain social separation and discipline in these shelters, enough police officers should be on hand. Police and revenue officials must know where all food and service centres are located, so they can direct migrant workers who are walking to them.

Service is the seventh item on the list

The Director of Social Welfare is said to be leading the effort. A more concentrated effort, however, is required by this Court. There should be a Nodal Officer of a high rank (Tahsildar/DSP etc.) appointed by each District Collector and Superintendent of Police to oversee and monitor the operations of each shelter and its residents. Each shelter should be examined by a Tahsildar and DSP. In the event of a staffing shortfall, the District Legal Services Authority's services are also available. The services of other organisations, such as the Para Legal Volunteers, NSS, NCC, the Bharath Scout and Guide Association, the

Red Cross, the Lions Club and the Rotary Club, should also be utilised in order to staff these shelters and ensure that the migrant workers receive food, medical care, and other necessities. The shelter's Nodal Officers will be tasked with coordinating all operations. For now, the State is picking up and transporting any migrant labourers who are strolling through the area. According to the counter-affidavit filed by the State, they have previously moved a significant number of intra and interstate migrant workers and are in the process of transferring others, both by train and bus, who are willing to return to their original location. It is proposed that these temporary solutions be used to support state efforts until the same is completed and mass road migration ceases. Efforts should be made to persuade migrant workers to use the state-funded transit instead of walking. Issues of quarantine, spread of COVID etc., are left up to the separate State authorities and this Court's Order will not interfere with the State's choice in any individual's instance to quarantine or restrict him from travelling. Interim orders, like this one, are simply meant to bolster existing efforts until mass labour migration is curbed.

By May 22, 2020, this Court must be informed on the implementation of temporary measures, including details of the shelters and services provided. As directed by the Court, follow-up reports should be filed on a regular basis.

(6) Japinder Singh v. U.O.I,[58]

Judges-C.J. Ramesh Rangnathan, J. R.C. Khulbe

Facts of the Case

On May 2, 2020, the State Government issued an order furthering its earlier ruling dated April 22, 2020, which allowed private unaided schools in the State to offer lessons online without a court permission. Private schools were barred from collecting any fees other than tuition under a government order issued on May 2, 2020. Only in circumstances when private unaided schools were providing online lessons for their pupils did this possibility for collecting tuition fees become available. No tuition fees may be collected from students at private unaided institutions that did not provide online lessons. Those schools, which were also expected to pay the wages of their professors and employees from their own finances, were ordered to rigorously conform to the directions provided in the Government Order dated May 2, 2020.

In this case, the petitioner, Japinder Singh complaint that Parents are being coerced to pay tuition fees by these private schools, even though the Government Order dated 2.05.2020 stated that parents had the option of paying for their children's education. Even these institutions claimed to be able to offer online lessons for pupils in the upper grades. He also stated that this scam is solely used to collect tuition payments from parents who are easily duped.

Schools sent out emails and WhatsApp messages urging parents to pay their children's tuition fees, despite the fact that the Government Order stated that such payments should be voluntary; additionally, because Uttarakhand is a hilly and poor state, many of its residents lack internet access, preventing their children from participating in the online classes offered by the schools, despite this, parents are being forced to pay these fees. Parents who are unable to pay their child's tuition must be given consideration for a tuition fee extension under the terms of the decree.

Observation

The court observed that schools were free to send notices for nonpayment of school fees, and parents may be given an opportunity to explain and resolve their financial issues before the school can pursue legal action if the explanation was not adequate.

Parents would be able to voice their concerns about school fees, and the State Government should appoint a Nodal Officer and make it clear that no private school should send email or whatsapp messages to the parents demanding fees, because payment of fees was voluntary and only be charged from students who were accessing online education.

They kept in mind that school authorities were also facing issues during this pandemic. Teachers and staff, establishment charges, rent for buildings, vehicle maintenance, Employee State Provident Fund, Employee State Insurance, for its employees were just a few of the many costs that these schools had to deal with on a day-to-day basis. The main objective of the court was to alleviate the financial burden of parents who cannot afford to pay the huge amount charged by the unaided educational institutions.

Held

Following conclusions had been made in this case:

Every district in the state will have a nodal officer that parents may go to with concerns about private schools pressuring them to pay tuition fees, and these officers would be appointed by the state government. The public at large in the state will be made aware of the existence of the Nodal Officers, who can be contacted in this respect.

On receiving any such complaints, the officers would take strict action towards those educational institutions who tried to forcing parents for the submission of fees. Only those children who were availing the online course had to give tuition fees, no other charges. Public schools should not send emails or whatsapp messages to parents demanding fees because payment is voluntary, and only those students who access online education will be charged, and the State Government should appoint a Nodal Officer and make this widely known so that parents can raise their grievances about the School Fees issue.

Conclusion

Here, the main objective of this judgement was to reduce the financial or mental burden of the parents and keeping in mind the issues faced by private educational institutions during lockdown because even schools and institutions had to pay teachers, principals and staff. COVID-19 made survival miserable for everyone and Courts were getting bombarded with multiple issues from everywhere. Therefore, the Hon'ble apex court worked wisely during such a period and delivered judgement that was favourable for every one.

(7) Amit Bhargava v. State of (NCT) Delhi and Ors.[59]

Judges- J. C Hari Shankar

Facts of the Case

Due to the worldwide COVID-19 pandemic, the Government of India announced a nation-wide lockdown on 24.03.2020 for a period of 21 days with effect from 25.03.2020. At that time, the number of cases were increasing day by day. The petitioner who was photojournalist by profession had allegedly come into contact with the delivery man on 24.03.2020, when the Petitioner ordered a food delivery.

The Delivery Person tested positive for COVID-19 on April 14, 2020. After that notice of Home Quarantine was posted on the Petitioner's dwelling door on April 15, 2020, from March 24, 2020, to April 20, 2020. A quarantine period of 28 days was in effect from the 24th of March until the 20th of April 2020.

The Petitioner is alleged to have ignored the quarantine notice and to have continued to quarantine itself. Once he received the warning, the quarantine staff informed him that he had violated quarantine guidelines. On April 15, the Petitioner received a letter notifying him that he had been quarantined for 14 days because he had been in contact with a person who had tested positive for corona. The Petitioner claims that this is not in accordance with applicable rules (i.e., Guidelines for Home Quarantine, issued on March 14, 2020). There had been more than 14 days since Petitioner's interaction with Delivery Boy when the quarantine notice was issued, according to Petitioner.

It is because of this that the petitioner contends that his quarantine has been prolonged in violation of the law. The petitioner also mentioned in his pray that covid 19 testing should be available in private labs for quarantined individuals, so they don't have to rely on government hospitals for free tests.

Observation

A writ court in India is prohibited from directing policy formulation by Article 226 of the Indian Constitution. The hon'ble court had also referred the case of **State of Himachal Pradesh VS Satpal Saini**[60] in which it was held that: "The courts do not frame policy or mandate that a particular policy should be followed. The duty to formulate policies is entrusted to the executive whose accountability is to the legislature and, through it, to the people." The Court points out that the petitioner's reasoning is not illogical. However, it must be evaluated. However, the Court acknowledges that in these situations, there is a constant trade-off between saving lives and preserving individual rights, but it states that the first part (saving lives) has the primacy.

Held

In this case, the Court believed that the 14-day timeframe specified in the Guidelines of the 14th of March had been viewed as merely informative. Because of this case, the Court stated that it "is unwilling to hold that in each and every case, the length of home quarantine must be restricted to 14 days, and no more".

However, quarantining an individual without a valid reason had harmful effects.

So the Court says "anyone who does not show symptoms of COVID-19, has not tested positive for the COVID-19 virus, and is quarantined for more than 14 days" should have "a right to represent authorities against such continued quarantine and, if he so represents authorities, they would be bound to lift quarantine as soon as possible and without undue delay".

The court had rejected the request made by the petitioner that covid 19 testing should been made available in private labs for quarantined individuals, so they don't have to rely on government hospitals for free tests by stating that there may be a variety of justifications for quarantining an individual.

Conclusion

The court had not gave its decision fully in favor but and had made a fair decision by giving statement that anyone who has not shown symptoms of COVID-19 or tested positive for the virus, and has been confined at home for more than 14 days, shall have a "right to represent to the authorities against such continued isolation.

The Court prudently worked upon its decisions as the circumstances and needs during different waves of Covid 19 changed. Hon'ble High Court kept in mind both center and state guidelines along with the one's issued by Hon'ble Supreme Court hence, maintaining a balance promoting co-operative federalism.

Footnotes

1 Indian Penal Code, 1860 S. 188, No. 45 Act of Parilament, 1860- It is not required that the offender want to do harm or that he or she considers his or her disobedience to be likely to cause harm before acting. That he is aware of the command that he is disobeying, and that his disobedience has caused or is likely to cause harm, is sufficient evidence of his guilt. Illustration

An order is proclaimed by a public servant who is legally authorised to do so, instructing that a religious procession must not travel through a specific street, and it is effective immediately. An individual who willfully disobeys an order and so increases the risk of rioting. As specified in this section, A has committed the offence defined in this section..

2 Indian Penal Code, 1860 S. 269, No. 45 Act of Parliament, 1860- Anyone who commits an unlawful or negligent act that is, and which he knows or has reason to believe, is likely to spread the infection of any disease that is life-threatening shall be punished with imprisonment of either description for a term that may be extended to six months, or with a fine, or with both, in addition to other penalties.

3 Indian Penal Code, 1860 S. 270, No. 45 Act of Parliament, 1860 Every act committed with malice that is, and which he knows or has cause to think, will spread the infection of any disease that is life-threatening will be punished by imprisonment of either sort for a time that may extend to two years, or by fine, or by either punishment alone.

4 Indian Penal Code, 1860 S. 271, No. 45 Act of Parliament, 1860 Disobedience to quarantine rule

5 Code of Criminal Procedure 1973, S. 144 No. 2 Act of Parliament, 1973- to enable the Magistrate to pass quick order and deal speedily where public nuisance or obstruction is made.

6 Disaster Management Act, 2005 S. 6 No. 53, Act of Parliament, 2005-The powers and functions of the National Authority. — The National Authority is responsible for formulating disaster management policies, strategies, and guidelines in accordance with the provisions of this Act in order to guarantee timely and effective disaster response. The National Authority may, without limiting the generality of the requirements of subsection (1), do any of the following: (a) establish catastrophe management policies; (b) ratify the National Plan; (c) approve plans submitted by Government of India Ministries or Departments that are in conformity with the National Plan; (c) establish guidelines for the State Authorities to follow in developing the State Plan; and

(e) establish guidelines for the various Ministries or Departments of the Government of India. (1) The National Power may delegate authority to the Chairperson of the National Authority to exercise all or some of the National Authority's responsibilities in the case of an emergency; however, such action must be approved by the National Authorityex post facto before it may be implemented.

7 Disaster Management Act, 2005 S. 10, No. 53, Act of Parliament, 2005)- A total of eleven authorities and functions are delegated to the National Executive Committee. (11) The National Executive Committee shallassist the National Authority in the discharge of its functions and shall be in charge of carrying out policies and plans developed by the National Authority and ensuring compliance with Central Government directives issued for the purpose of disaster management in the country. (2) The National Executive Committee shall be in charge of ensuring compliance with Central Government directives issued for disaster management in the country. The National Executive Committee may, without limiting the scope of the provisions of sub-section (1), perform the following functions: (a) act as the primary coordinating and monitoring body for disaster management; (b) prepare the National Plan, which must be approved by the National Authority; (c) coordinate and monitor the implementation of the National Policy; and (d) lay down guidelines for different Ministries or Departments of the Government of India in order to prepare disaster management plans.

8 Disaster Management Act, 2005 S. 38, No. 53, Act of Parliament, 2005- In this case, the state government will take the necessary steps. Each state government, subject to the provisions of this Act, is obligated to carry out all of the procedures outlined in the guidelines issued by the National Authority, as well as any extra activities it deems necessary or expedient, for the purpose of disaster management. (2) The measures that the State Government may take under sub-section (1) may relate to all or any of the following matters: (a) coordination of actions of different departments of the State

Government, the State Authority, District Authorities, local authorities, and other non-governmental organisations; (b) cooperation and assistance in disaster management to the National Authority and National Executive Committee, the State Authority, and other non-governmental organisations; and (c) cooperation and assistance in disaster management to the National Authority and National Executive Committee, the State Authority, and other non-governmental In addition, the State Government must: (e) ensure that departments of the State Government incorporate disaster prevention and mitigation measures into their development plans and projects; (f) incorporate into the State development plan measures to reduce or mitigate different parts of the State's vulnerability to different disasters; and (g) ensure that different departments of the State Government prepare disaster management plans in accordance with the guidelines laid out by the National Disaster Management Organization..

9 Disaster Management Act, 2005 S. 72, No. 53, Act of Parliament, 2005.

10 Disaster Management Act, 2005 , No. 53, Act of Parliament, 2005.

11 India Const. art. 21

12 India Const. art. 39, cl. (e), As stated in Article 39(e), the state is responsible for ensuring that "the health and strength of employees, both men and women, and the delicate age of children" are neither harmed or neglected.

13 India Const., art. 41.

14 India Const., art. 42.

15 India Const., art. 47.

16 India Const., art. 246

17 According to the High-Level Expert Group (HLEG), primary health care should be a top priority, and funds should be allocated to provide general healthcare information and promotion, primary care therapeutic services, population health risk testing, and possible treatmentswhich are both financially feasible and focused at particular risk factors.

18 141 1-15th Finance commission- "Finance Commission in COVID Times", (2020)

19 India Const., art.38.

20 Patel, Bimal N. *"National Security of India and International Law."* NSIL. (2020).

21 Pashchim Banga Khet Maxdoor Samity and Ors. V. The State of West Bengal, (1996) 4 SCC 37.

22 CESC Limited v. Subhash Chandra Bose AIR 1992 SCC 37.

23 T. RamaKrishan Rao v. Hyderabad Development Authority- 2002 (2) ALT 193.

24 The Constitution of India, 1950, Art. 21

25 The Constitution of India, 1950, Art. 47

26 Ratlam Municipal Council v. Vardichand Air 1980 SC 1622.

27 Keshvananda Bharti v. State of Kerala (1973) 4 SCC 225.

28 Pt. Parmanand Katara vs Union of India (1989) AIR 2039

29 AIR 1984 SC 112.

30 The Constitution of India, 1950.

31 Powers and responsibilities of the National Authority However, without limiting the generality of the provisions contained in sub-section (1), the National Authority may take any other measures it deems necessary for the prevention of disaster, mitigation of disaster, or preparation and capacity building for dealing with a threatening disaster situation or disaster.

32 The Ministry of Health and Family Welfare is a government ministry in India that is responsible for the country's health policies. The organisation is also in charge of all government initiatives in India that are related to family planning. Because she is a member of the Council of Ministers, she has cabinet status and is responsible for health and family welfare policy.

33 The Pradhan Mantri Garib Kalyan Yojana, or the Pradhan Mantri Garib Kalyan Scheme, 2016, a plan announced by the Indian government in December 2016 and modelled after the Income

Declaration Scheme, 2016, which was launched earlier in theyear, is a new type of taxation system.

34 A piece of PPE, often called "PPE," is any part of gear which is dressed to decrease risk exposures that might cause serious injuries or illnesses on the job. These injuries & illnesses can be caused by chemical, radioactive, physical, electrical, mechanical, as well as other kinds of workplace possible risks.

35 (1998) 4 SCC 117.

36 Supra note 1.

37 Ibid.

38 The Central Government's Authority. After determining that India or any part of it is being visited by or threatened with an outbreak of any dangerous epidemic disease and that the ordinary provisions of the law currently in force are insufficient to prevent such outbreak or spread, the Central Government may take measures and prescribe regulations for the inspection of any ship or vessel departing or arriving at any port in India, including the port of Chennai.

39 Mokbul Ali Laskar- "Dynamics of Indian Federalism: A Comprehensive Historical Review" (pp 120-121 Notion Press 2015).

40 Anandi Shukla, Rai, Balram, and Laxmi Kant Dwivedi- "*COVID-19 in India: predictions, reproduction number and public health preparedness.*" MedRxiv (2020).

41 Supra 8

42 Matthew M., Kavanagh, and Renu Singh et. Al.- *"Democracy, capacity, and coercion in pandemic response: COVID-19 in comparative political perspective."* JHPPL (2020).

43 Persons operating in accordance with the Act are protected. Nothing in this Act shall give rise to a claim or other legal action against any person for anything done or intended to be done in good faith in violation of this Act.

44 The "Health Services Personnel and Clinical Establishments (Prohibition of Violence and Property Damage) Bill, 2019",

which made unlawful assault to healthcare workers like doctors, nursing staff, as well as paramedics and called for a maximum five-year prison sentence alongwith a fine of 5 lakh for violators, was withdrawn recently.

45 The Constitution of India, 1950.

46 As per the Directive Principles, the state is obligated to enhance public health by raising the level of nutrition and living standards, among other things. In particular, the state is required to work toward the ban of intoxicating beverages and narcotics, which is a priority duty.

47 The Constitution of India, 1950.

48 The Public Health (Prevention, Control, and Management of Epidemics, Bioterrorism, and Disasters) Bill, 2017

49 Abraham P ,Aggarwal N ,Babu GR et al.- "*Laboratory surveillance for SARS-CoV-2 in India: performance of testing & descriptive epidemiology of detected COVID-19, January 22–April 30, 2020.*" Indian J Med Res. (2020).

50 Chatterjee P ,Anand T ,Singh KJ et al."*Healthcare workers & SARS-CoV-2 infection in India: a case-control investigation in the time of COVID-19.*" Indian J Med Res. (2020).

51 India Const. art. 21- Article 21 guarantees two rights: 1) The right to life; and 2) the right to personal liberty 52 M.A. 665 of 2021.

53 Ibid.

54 Suo Moto W.P. 3 of 2021.

55 W.P. 01

56 W.P. 10983 of 2020.

57 W.P. 101 of 2020.

58 W.P. 59 of 2020.

59 W.P. (C) 3016 of 2020.

60 Ibid.

04
CHAPTER

NATIONAL LOCKDOWN – AN APPROACH TO CO-OPERATIVE FEDERALISM

4.1 Background

As the Constitution of India divides the powers and duties among Centre and State by the virtue of Union List, State List, and Concurrent List, the said division of powers helps in smooth governance, management and implementation of policy throughout the nation. The State List, entries 1 and 2 designate legislative realms such as "public policy," "police," and, perhaps most crucially, "public health and health-related institutions, hospitals, and districts" while Entry 23 & 29 of the Concurrent List assigns the area of "social security" to the Member States. Articles 73 and 162 of the Constitution stipulate that the Union and its states have "coextensive with legislative power" in their administrative functions. State authorities are expected to take the initiative in public health and law enforcement, whereas the central govt. is tasked with offering overall national leadership, enabling cooperation between many important federal units, tracking the overall pandemic scenario, and offering financial as well as other essential help and support to states.

Immediately following the disaster that struck India in early March of 2020, the central and state administrations gave two alternatives for legislation. As per the "Disaster Management Act, 2005" the Union declared the pandemic a "notified disaster" and ordered a state-wide lockdown on March 24, 2020, to limit the outbreak. Despite the fact that the term "disaster" does not appear in the Act's seventh schedule, the Union has frequently used it in its responses to the pandemic's spread and given orders to states. The states used various parts of the 1860 penal code to impose sanctions on violators before the Centre established its own rules for doing so. But it has been discovered that many of the current procedures aimed at ensuring an effective government response to the pandemic have been shown to be inadequate in many instances. The current legislation's safeguards were deemed to be inadequate since it was either inherited from colonial precedents or was not specifically designed to work with a pandemic catastrophe in modern times. When faced with a severe problem like COVID-19, a modern targeted all-encompassing legal framework was required. Something that was clearly lacking at the time. The Union and states were required to employ regulations to address any constitutional and legal flaws.

4.2 Introduction

Government is the group of political and legal organizations which control how people in a society interact with each other and with people from outside the society. These groups have the power to make decisions on behalf of society about policies that affect the maintenance of order and the achievement of certain community goals. A government's power over its citizens varies depending on how liberated it is from restrictions and restraints while the number of personnel and material resources it has at its disposal determines how effective its foreign policy will be.

We as Indians have long debated the merits of federal vs unitary constitutions as our has both a federal and a unitary constitutional system. A complete understanding of the distinction between federal and unitary is necessary before coming to any conclusion.

4.2.1 Characteristics of Federal Structure of Indian Constitution

There are certain features of Indian Constitution which makes it federal/quasi federal in nature. The said features are:

1. **Supremacy of Constitution:** An important federal aspect of India's constitution is that 'the constitution has supreme authority'. This supremacy necessitates conformity at all levels

of govt., including the federal and state levels. In addition, the constitution establishes separate but equal powers for the state and federal govts.

2. **Written Constitution:** A written form of a federal constitution is necessary for it to be effective. The Indian Constitution is the most comprehensive written constitution in existence. One of the key elements of federalism is rigorous constitutionalism, which the Indian constitution embodies.

3. **Rigid:** Constitutional amendments in a federal system are often subject to a lengthy and cumbersome process. A two-thirds majority is needed to ratify amendments to the Indian Constitution. To pass such an amendment, it must receive the support of 2/3 of the members of each house of parliament who were in attendance. However, some changes can only be put into effect if at least half of the states agree to them. The amendment is signed by the President of India after this process.

4. **Distribution of Powers:** The powers of the state and the center under India's constitution are clearly defined, as are the boundaries of the center and the state's legislative authority. The Union, the State, and the Concurrent List are all listed in our constitution. In all, there are 97 issues on the Union List that are of national significance. There are 66 topics on the State List, all of which are relevant to a certain community. Subjects such as Electricity, Trade Union, Economic and Social Planning, and so forth, are included in the Concurrent List of 47.

5. **Judicial Supremacy and Judicial Independence:** In a federal system with a separate court to interpret the Constitution and uphold its integrity, the supremacy of the judiciary is a critical characteristic. In cases involving the Union and its states, the Supreme Court of India has exclusive jurisdiction.

   If a statute violates the Constitution in any way, it can be declared unconstitutional by the apex court.

In the case of "Rajasthan v. Union of India," Professor Wheare's theory of federalism was utilised to describe the Indian constitution as "more unitary than federal." He continued by saying that the Indian union is somewhat federal. However, the scope of federalism is severely constrained by the pressing necessity for a country to evolve and develop, which necessitates national integration, economic coordination, and social, intellectual, and spiritual elevation. It was for these reasons that Art. 356's exercise of central authority was deemed necessary. "Karnataka v. Union of India"[1] CJ Beg, once again said that notwithstanding any federalism in the framework of our constitution, 'unitary aspects' were also there. Specifically, this was done to refute the state's claim that the federal principle was infringed by the center conducting investigations into the behavior of state ministers. Thus, the dual function of the governor of a state, as the state's constitutional head as well as an agent of the federal government, and his capacity to announce a constitutional break down in the state's machinery leading to its overthrow by the union government.

The union's dominant position has been further strengthened by its constitutional ability to give state governments the directives necessary to ensure compliance with national legislation enacted by the federal parliament. Articles 249, 352 to 360, and 371 are the primary reasons why India should have a quasi-federal constitution. The Rajmannar Committee was the first in India to study center-state relations in 1969. It pointed out that the development of unitary trends in India was caused by the states' financial dependence on the center. A similar position was expressed in the West Bengal Memorandum, approved by the West Bengal government, which said that the constitution made the centre a more dominating partner than the states. It is undeniable that the Indian Constitution places a greater emphasis on the central government than on the individual states.

4.2.2 Concept and Terminology

Before initiating with this chapter, it is important to understand the certain concept and terminology.

- **Lockdown:** During an emergency, individuals are prohibited from leaving a certain location. In the event of a complete lockdown, one is unable to leave or enter the designated area. In such situations, critical supplies are made available through the help of governmental agencies. All non-essential businesses and services are also restricted from opening in such situation.

Therefore, such a circumstance of isolation and restraint is known as Lockdown.

- **Federalism:** The Latin word "foedus," which means "covenant, contract, and treaty," is the root of the term "federalism." Federalism is a term for a type of governmental system wherein the nationwide government as well as the state govts. share power.

  A govt. is made up of two parts that work together. The federal govt. and the many state governments both have some power. "Separation of Power" is the guiding concept of various kinds of governments. A two-tiered system of federalism governs India, with the central government holding the reins of power and state governments exercising that authority at the local level. While the Indian Constitution calls for a parliamentary system of government, it also has federal and unitary elements. Legislative, executive, and judicial authority are the three main pillars of the federal government.

- **Cooperative Federalism**: It is a philosophy that aims to keep things running well between union and state government. States, Panchayat Raj Entities, and Urban Local Bodies should all work together to accomplish common objectives for the good of society. States disregard the values of federalism when it comes to power sharing with local authorities. In India, local and state govts. actually, work together in a way that is not based on the idea of federalism. Because of this, there is a need to study the interactions between states and between states and local governments.

4.2.3 Co-operative Federalism in India and Why India followed it

Federation is the division of a nation into a central government and multiple subordinate governments, such as states, provinces, regional governments and other similar bodies. Working together to address common problems is an important part of this form of federalism. Co-operative Federalism can form this link between the state and national govts. through the use of money in kind or cash, influencing policy or norm (Ex: freight equalisation policy, SEZs etc.), creating critical motorways or similar corridors, etc. for initiatives. The federal govt.

could issue grants in aid—a particular type of grant from the federal govt. which provides funds for states to adopt a policy—to assure that national roadways are adequately maintained. Grant money may be used to pay for elements or supplies, or to compensate for the actual road construction project's contractors and staff. Under Art. 263 of constitution, there is a provision for establishing an Inter-State Council for the purpose of coordinating relations between the federal government and each of its constituent states. As part of the State Reorganization Act of 1956, the Zonal Councils were established as another institutional tool for interstate and inter-state cooperation. The "National Development Council (NDC)" and "the National Integration Council (NIC)" are the other two key platforms for debate and the resolution of conflicts of opinion. Various ministries have established central councils in order to improve coordination.

Invoking the phrase "federalism" brings to mind images of democracy, progress, the constitution, and other lofty ideals. The goal of federalism is to bring together two distinct groups of people by using different institutional mechanisms of 'shared governance'. Center-state interactions and state autonomy have therefore become major problems in Indian federalism for the reasons stated above. It was meant to be a snub to the Sarkaria Commission's establishment in 1983 by the union government, Indian Federalism was examined by the Commission, but no recommendations were made on how to build Indian federalism effectively. Several recommendations from this panel were also implemented by the federal government in a very sluggish manner. However, even though our constitution is supposedly federal, this overemphasis on the federal government renders it unable to properly deal with socioeconomic issues and build national unity. That is why restructuring Indian Federalism is necessary in order to improve its effectiveness and foster the center-state relationship.

India promoted the doctrine of Co-operative Federalism due to its advantages and it being the supporting system of Constitutional Framework. The said advantages are-

(i) **Decentralization of Powers-** The Panchayat (local government) in India is the source of power in the country's administration. In order to avoid a unitary system of government, decentralization is required to prevent the centre from acquiring all authority,

(ii) **Smooth and Simple governance-** The overworked administration benefits from the use of this method. In India, there are three levels of government: the executive, legislative, and judicial. Villages are out of reach for the top execs. Consequently, the local government serves as a bridge between the executive and the people, allowing them to participate in democracy at a lower level,

(iii) **Maintenance of Constitutional Supremacy-** Under contrast to unitary administration, where supremacy rests with Parliament, in a federal system, the Constitution remains the highest law of the nation. The laws of the land are carefully enforced. Constitutional primacy extends to India as well,

(iv) **Quasi Federal Status-** All of the government's authority is held by the central government under a Unitary type of government. Most of the authority belongs with the central government under this sort of political system. Both the United Kingdom and Sri Lanka are governed by a single system of law. In many instances, the larger government in India is completely subordinate to the union government. As a quasi-federal state, India's central government has greater authority during times of emergency than the state governments. The Centre and the State do not have the same amount of power and

(v) **Emergency-** Central and State governments may violate on each other's territory in the case of emergency or public safety, although this isn't permitted. The federal government's legislation always take precedence over state or local ones in the Concurrent List. Under Article 352, 356 and 360, during the time of declaration of emergency federal government becomes more powerful than the State Government and state loses its autonomy.

In times of crisis, India's system exhibits a unitary characteristic that undermines federalism.

4.3 Co-Operative Federalism and COVID-19

In the aftermath of COVID-19, Indian federalism was put to the test as a means of coping with the effects of an economic downturn as well as large-scale migration. Government was not able to provide proper medical facilities in the midst of rising cases of COVID and hence, Lockdown was seemed to be as best possible resort to control the given situation. As visited in previous chapters that government handed over the power, conduct and deciding rules of said Lockdown to respective states, the present chapter of thesis shall study how National Lockdown was strategically devised approaching the united co-operative federalism and working within the nation. The pandemic response's early phases revealed India's federal structure's unitary leaning. Cooperative federalism looks to be emerging as the crisis deepens. But the absence of coordination among Centre & States unwillingness to enable horizontal federalism without involving any international body has made migrant workers' life hellish. The Inter-State Council (ISC) serves as a shared platform for the federal government and the states to work together smoothly. The potential of India's base level of governance was also brought to light, but it was underutilized.

The Constitution of India allows for the decentralization of public services such as drinking water, healthcare, elementary education, and interstate highways. Because of the Union's disinterest and some states' intentional inability to execute compulsory functional, financial, as well as administrative decentralisation, local democracy has reported a serious loss over the past quarter-century.[2] Local democracy has progressed slowly and unevenly, with the exception of some states like Kerala. Our federation's prosperity rests as much on amicable and cooperative links between the individual States as it does on the connection between the Centre and states. Inter-State ties have been plagued by a number of issues, including the recent coronavirus pandemic. As a result of the federal government's incapacity to create horizontal federalism in the absence of a competent interstate agency, conditions for migrant workers have gotten worse. These issues seem to have intensified owing to the lack of multilateral organisations. During the pandemic, informal cross-border exchange has undoubtedly grown. According to some scholars, the Inter-State Council (ISC) may have functioned as a platform for the federal government and the states to collaborate in both a vertical and horizontal manner under the said one umbrella. In truth, it has never been put to use to its fullest extent. Because of this, despite what the government has declared, it has not brought back the ISC, as has been pointed out. To date, the ISC has only met 11 times in the past three decades. Constitution clearly defines the tasks and responsibilities of municipal and regional governments as well as the federal and state governments.

While other countries struggled to contain the Covid-19 outbreak, India demonstrated a strong central leadership role. State and local governments did have to suffer because of a strong central government. Indian federalism was put to the test as a result of the COVID-19 outbreak in the global financial crisis and the growing complexity of a multi-level constitutional framework. Cooperative federalism may be seen ascending to the vertical plane as time went on. Migrant labourer's life was made a misery by the State's lack of collaboration and coordination. It was also debatable if the Centre had a role in facilitating horizontal federalism.

In order to deal with an outbreak in a nation with highly populated, where religious, social, & political meetings are a routine part of daily life, and also where large-scale interstate migration happens, the federal govt., the states, and local authorities had to work together. Experts across the globe were worried that India wouldn't be able to handle this. State and federal governments took a variety of actions as the outbreak of COVID-19 began to spread in mid-March. Several states enacted partial lockdowns and closed their borders as a precautionary measure. The GoI declared a three-week countrywide lockdown on 24th March 2020, limiting the freedom of movement for the country's 1.35 billion citizens for the duration of the lockdown. Most states were unprepared for the four-hour notice of the country-wide lockdown. The repatriation of migrant workers to their home countries was extremely problematic.

State administrations, did not object to the Central government's move considering the fact that entire nation was facing such a situation for the first time in history and the states as well as centre had no resort left other than adopting the lockdown instantaneously due to massive spread of disease, opinion of state under normal circumstances would have caused a significant political flashpoint. The federal and state governments implemented a series of lockdowns throughout the months of May, June, and July, each with a different level of restriction. Coordination and cooperation between India's states and the Union (Central) government have been key to the country's response to

COVID-19. Because no one authority or level of government can handle the situation on their own, the pandemic has highlighted the need to promote cooperative federalism. In 2020,[3] this cooperative aspect of federalism may have been on show during the earliest stages of the lockdown during Covid 19, but later on it emerged as more of a top-down strategy, rather. The Central administration was heavily criticised for their decision by the States. However, with the passage of time, things began to shift. Before giving instructions for the prolongation of lockdown, the Central Government was compelled to initiate negotiations with the chief ministers of several States. The states gained more and more influence in the process of making decisions. Containment zones can only be established by state govt., and those govt. are now in charge of deciding which areas qualify as such.

Before the second lockdown, the Hon'ble Prime Minister of the nation held a videoconference meeting with the CMs of all Indian states. As a result of states responding to the call for collaboration, healthcare facilities improved. N-95 face masks, PPE kits, as well as ventilators were imported by India, but today the country is practically self-sufficient and can export them. At the same time, those in need who had lost their means of support due to the outbreak received financial assistance from government. All three levels of government have been found to be active in their respective fights against pandemic, although to differing degrees of success and efficiency. First and foremost, the capability of States or UTs and their PH infrastructure was crucial. States like Kerala, Karnataka, and Orissa, which have lower populations, have been able to better manage their resources. Local governments had an important role as well because it possessed full responsibility over public health in the metropolitan region. BMC in Mumbai is an example to the "Dharavi model," which refers to their effective engagement in reducing the pandemic in Dharavi (slum), a densely populated district of Mumbai, which was widely recognised both locally and globally. A phenomenal aspect of State co-ordination with local government was shown in Dharavi region of Mumbai.[4]

India achieved a number of notable milestones as a result of collaboration between the federal & state govt. India came in 2nd in the world after the US in terms of how many tests they did. The findings of a nationwide survey of Covid-19 diagnostic laboratories were startling.[5]

Even in low-income states like Jharkhand, Bihar, and Madhya Pradesh, infrastructure was improved and COVID-19 labs were constructed in each district. In India, there were 93 deaths per million people, compared to 749 deaths per million people in the United States and over 750 deaths per million people in European countries including the United Kingdom, Spain, and Italy. According to WHO, India's achievements in combatting the pandemic will be recognized in 2020, and an example of the same may be seen here -" *While there were just 14 labs in February, there were more than 1596 by August, an increase of more than 700 percent. The rate of testing has increased considerably in the recent few months due to the addition of the rapid antigen detection test to the molecular tests, which remain the major diagnostic tool, according to the World Health Organization (WHO) in 2020.* At the highest echelons of government, there was a general consensus. Despite this, there were noteworthy anomalies, like the declaration of a countrywide lockdown on March 24, 2020, with little previous consultation or notification. The virus had to be contained while the economic effects of the lockdown were being dealt with by the state/UT and municipal administrations. After a few weeks, the central government finally got involved. Pandemic-related concerns including as lockdowns, migrant workers' conditions, and budget constraints have all raised questions about what it means to practise 'cooperative federalism.' Next, we'll go into more depth about each of these difficulties.

Under the jurisdiction of the EDA (1897), state govts. made a number of plans to separate people by social class and make it harder for people to move around. Under the law, people who did not followed orders made under the EDA were punished. Curfews and restrictions on public gatherings were permitted under Criminal Procedure Code (CrPC) of 1973. Accordingly, states and the federal govt. first implemented strict containment measures, such as lockdowns, in specific locations. As a result, district-level policies must be documented in order to accurately account for subnational reactions. The following are the classifications there-

(a) **Announcement of a Pandemic:** By recognizing the scenario an emergency and making it official, the govt. sends a message to its people to get ready for preventive actions.

(b) **Closures:** Closing numerous services and limiting the operation of various institutions has been a fundamental method to ensure social estrangement. This category includes four measurements:

(i) Academic establishment closures

(ii) Restaurants & pubs closures

(iii) Community centres closures like theatre, museums, gymnasiums, etc.

(iv) Non-essential services closures of private business organisations, retail, and government agencies

(c) **Internal Travel Limits:** The social distancing policy also includes travel restrictions & public transportation. It includes 2 measures:

(i) Public transportation restrictions like cabs, buses, trains, & aeroplanes

(ii) All borders are closed, and all interstate transit, particularly private transport, is prohibited.

(d) **Public Gathering Restrictions:** Many governments have imposed a restriction on public gathering in order to maintain social isolation. This effectively imposes a limit on the total number of people who can gather in a given area, such as a park or a special event such as wedding.

4.4 India's Status Quo and Co-Operative Federalism during Different Waves of COVID-19

4.4.1 1st Wave – The Ruckus between Central Unilateral Approach and State Autonomy

If there is a crisis like the COVID-19 outbreak, the center government has the primary responsibility for resolving it. As a result, the Center was in charge of the outbreak and led from the front during the statewide curfew period (24th March – 31st May 2020). When the pandemic endangered the lives and livelihoods of millions of people, the Center took on responsibilities that would ordinarily fall within the purview of the state government in order to coordinate a rapid response across the country. Several extensive measures have been adopted including a set of options for increasing vaccination purchases and gathering data for the development of regulations and guidelines for local & state govt., as well as reducing cross-state externalities.[6] On March 24, 2020, the Center took the decision on its own to put a lockdown on the whole country. Even though it told the state govts. what the risk was, the Centre decided to lockdown the whole nation with only four hours' notice.

The Centre's power came from the DMA (2005)[7]. While this was being implemented, there was no national plan in place to help mitigate the negative effects of such severe limitations on movement. Additionally, the Center utilised other sections of the DMA in order to instruct the states on how long the lockdown should remain, how many individuals should be inside, and where they should be held.[8] MHA has overall responsibility for recommending and implementing lockdown measures and related limitations across India under the DMA, which came into effect in 2012.[9]

One of the most significant criticisms levelled at the Center's initial response to the outbreak was the unannounced implementation of a state-wide lockdown, which was essential at the time. Refugees fleeing to rural areas without jobs or the necessities of life had to travel great distances. There was a humanitarian crisis left to handled by state governments, which were taken aback by the flood of their own migratory workers who were returning home. These workers had been away for some time.[10] The states couldn't buy medical supplies on their own due economic crisis and moreover Centre's approval was required anyways. These were some of the hindrances states faced while dealing with the medical requirement of their region. This had an effect on the states' capacity to mobilise and augment crucial resources.[11] Many times, the MHA sent supervision teams to states without contacting the particular state governments, which was a violation of state sovereignty.[12] As a result, the early phase of the pandemic brought the full range of the Centre's powers to the fore: *"it was the Centre that imposed the lockdown, and it was also the Centre that monitored state responses, including physical-distancing norms, regulation of economic activities, and provision of financial packages."*[13] Key state responsibilities and authorities such as restricting liquor sales and stopping (or resuming) public transit were also assumed by the federal government during the lockdown period, which sparked an uproar from the states.

Once the MHA pushed the Kerala state govt. to reverse its judgement to permit eateries to operate based on its local assessment, it was perhaps the pinnacle of "centralised federalism."[14] Finally, after a lot of pressure from the states, the federal government relinquished its authority over COVID-19 because it became evident that central control was a major impediment to its containment.[15]

Centralization in India's early reaction to COVID-19 was characterised by budgetary centralization. State governments were often left at the mercy of the federal government, which had a monopoly on scarce financial resources. In terms of taxing authority and associated domains, India's federal arrangement does indeed have a "central leaning." Some financial instruments that the states have valid rights on were seized by the Centre during the pandemic.[16] The first round of discussion was spurred by the payment of INR 300 billion in Goods and Services Tax (GST) to states. While the lockdown and other interruptions were causing financial hardship for the states, the federal government delayed the payment of GST earnings for many months, prompting the states to make serious warnings about the situation.[17] Since there was a severe shortage of public funds and states were scrambling to raise more funds, the arbitrary nature of the federal government became more apparent. There was a preference for conditional loans rather than unconditional relief handouts from the Centre, which was the necessity. State governments were forced to work with the federal government since they had little resources and no alternative except to accept temporary loss of authority and autonomy.[18]

4.4.2 Status of Co-operative Federalism during 2nd Wave

The Union's early response to the outbreak was marked by unilateralism and a distinctly centralised nature. This hasn't been the case during 2nd wave of the pandemic. As per the definition of Louise Tillin, "India has gone from unilateral central decision-making in the first wave to something that approximates unilateral decentralised decision-making—by default." First off, during the first wave of the crisis, the federal government acted swiftly and firmly. However, the Centers for "Disease Control and Prevention" proclaimed a nationwide lockdown and sent real-time information, orders, and procedures to state officials while many states implemented lockdowns and various physical separations methods. Medical supplies and PPE kits were able to be found and created in an incredibly short period of time thanks to the coordinated efforts of a government leadership that is committed to the future. Furthermore, the 2nd wave, which was more contagious and started overloading state healthcare systems as well as the national healthcare systems, demonstrated that the most of these Central efforts were futile.

Medical experts and the government's own scientific advisory body have predicted that a new and deadlier strain will emerge in January 2021, but the central government and its authorised agencies have taken no action in response to these predictions. Early in March 2021, the "Union Health Minister" said that the pandemic had come to an end in India.[19] The Kumbh Mela and election campaigns in five states were permitted to go forward despite health experts' concerns, while the central leadership engaged themselves with enormous demonstrations without pandemic-suitable restrictions. When a number of states began to experience substantial surges in infections and health systems began to crumble, the government would begin to take notice of the issue and respond accordingly.

PM's addressed the nation, calling for COVID-appropriate behaviour and for officials to rapidly escalate their response to the crisis.[20] A "state breakdown" was already in progress when they discovered the illnesses had quickly spread throughout the nation. When some state administrations publicly competed over crucial medications and oxygen cylinders, some blocked the deliveries of others, this became evident As interstate coordination broke down to such an extreme degree, the Supreme Court stepped in to break the impasse between the warring nations.[21]

It wasn't the federal government's duty to assist the states during a time of national crisis; instead, it attacked them for being complacent and saying that health was a state issue. A national lockdown and procedures and instructions on treatment and logistics were not issued quickly enough by the Centre, which expressed a reluctance to adopt drastic steps such as a national lockdown (even in a more critical scenario than the first wave). Localized control measures were left up to each state, which they very reluctantly approved in the first wave. Outright centralization was replaced by unilateral decentralisation as a result of this shift. In the vaccine policy, the decentralisation rationale became increasingly apparent. Because of the nation's vaccination crisis and the Central Govt. unexpected decision to expand the vaccination coverage from eighteen to forty-four yrs. of age, many state govt. sought independence to obtain vaccines from international markets. Due to a lack of vaccinations available and the fierce rivalry for vaccines, experts decided to accept the proposal.[22] Several governments that went through with vaccine procurement auctions were unable to find any bidders. As a result of this and deferential pricing of vaccinations, India's federal structure became a controversial issue. The Supreme Court had to intervene to break the impasse between state & federal govt.[23] Hence, "the Serum Institute" in Pune (India) and "Bharat Biotech" (India) were given the green light to employ Covishield and Covaxin vaccines for the 2020 mass immunisation campaign. According to the plan developed by the "Center for Disease Control and Prevention (CDC&P)", vaccines were procured from the respective manufacturing companies and then shipped to the states, where they were used to administer vaccinations to first frontline staff, then seniors, and eventually the population above 45 yrs. of age.

Union government has highest priority for the pandemic, although certain opposition-controlled states have made unreasonable requests on vaccine supply & some of them politicised the Canter's vacillation on vaccination to hide their incapability in dealing with the outbreak.[24] Eventually, following a long and acrimonious blame game, the Centre reversed its decision to assume charge of the vaccine campaign in early June. While the deadlock between the state and federal govt. on vaccination was resolved, the nation missed the early advantage of purchasing immunizations and expediting the deployment that was crucial to properly ending the outbreak.

4.4.3 Third Wave and Strengthened Co-operative Federalism

By the advent of third wave, the government was completely prepared with curbing down shortage of vaccines and hence, the states were moving ahead with limited restraints. Restrictions were imposed on specific bodies while not affecting the day-to-day life. By January 21, 2021 when 3,47,254 infections were detected, the third wave of COVID-19 had reached a stalemate in India. Ex-Center for Advanced Research in Virology director John says it is safe to infer that the third wave has terminated and India has entered an endemic phase once again.[25]

The major help was given by the panchayats (rural bodies) and urban local bodies during the process which have emerged as unsung heroes in the middle of the Center-State tussles in handling the pandemic. Many governments have transferred significant authority and responsibility to these third-tier organisations, despite the Center's repeated calls for their engagement in the pandemic response.[26] For instance, the govt of Odisha has granted the sarpanch the power of a magistrate to control the movement of migrants and enforce rules about physical distance. In the same way, the govt of Kerala let local groups do contact traceability, health programs, and clean-up projects, as well as teach people about how to stay healthy. Agricultural operations were supported by village local administrations, which ensured a steady supply of workers and essential food supply lines.[27] During the initial surge of the pandemic, district-level initiatives were effective in Bhilwara (Rajasthan), Agra (Uttar Pradesh), as well as Pathanamthitta (Kerala). All through the course of the outbreak, cities in states such as Maharashtra, in which the COVID-19 pandemic has been the most serious, adopted creative crisis management tactics.

4.4.4 Difficulties Faced during Co-operative Federalism

COVID-19 disease outbreak constituted significant challenges, such as the imposition of pan-India guidelines on issues that were rigidly the responsibility of the states, the complete ban of alcohol, the refusal of GST compensation, the irregular procurement of essential diagnostic instruments during the early lockdown phase, and the refusal of State disaster funds from the advantage of CSR contributions. Because of a lack of testing kits from the federal government, some states were unable to begin testing sooner. Several state reacted angrily to the 'red' and 'orange' designations of a region. It was attributed that, a day-long curfew and a state-wide lockdown were rushed implemented by the Central Govt., when only a few verified COVID-19 instances were being reported each day, according to several critics[28]. The ten-week lockdown, with only a few minor tweaks, disrupted most economic operations and severely limited the movement of people, resulting in considerable misery. Migrant workers in major cities have no way to return to their home states due to the initial suspension of transportation infrastructure. Thousands of people walked thousands of miles to get home, as has been widely reported. Concerns have been expressed regarding the Centre's readiness before it was announced that people would be forced to trek for days to get home. It was heartbreaking to see the misery of children, pregnant mothers, and migrants who were sleeping on train tracks. It was to their own detriment that the poor had been forgotten. Seeing and reading about the plight of migrant labourers has been a harrowing experience. They couldn't figure out a way to aid the thousands of individuals who were stuck in traffic. In this way, India's cooperative federalism failed miserably. State or UTs and local governments had to act quickly to help both local people and migrant workers with short term solutions such as accommodation, food, as well as other help (both PRs & municipal). The Rajasthan government stated that several states were delaying their permission for buses to enter their territory.[29] Special Shramik trains were then put in place by the government. These trains provided a means of transportation for migrants going back to their home states from May to July 2020.

Migrants were sent back to their home states via bus in certain States based on their own arbitrary determinations. Health services in rural regions were particularly concerned about the return of migrants because of the potential for new illnesses. A displeasure was expressed with respect to states that returned migrant labourers to Bihar back on buses. It was found to be contradictory to the point of the lockdown to shuttle thousands of people to Bihar.[30] Because migrants had worked in many states, some states argued that it was the obligation of those states to care for them which unfortunately, did not take place. Several states, including Haryana, Kerala, and Telangana, hosted camps for said labour. Lockdown Phase 1 should have implemented with a four- to five-day prior notice so that as many migrants as possible could have arrived at their destination. A few states also wanted to know why special trains ran so late and in such small numbers. In order to stop the trafficking of migrants, several states gave away free rides on special buses called "Shramik". Increasing the danger of infection was extensively highlighted in the media since employees were not transferred with social distance in mind. Vulnerable migrants seemed to be overlooked at first, but this has now changed. The "Shramik Special Trains" were only introduced when significant numbers of migrants collected at railway and bus terminals and began trekking hundreds of kilometres to their homes in the lack of transit. However, the absence of national planning led to the demise of those trains as well. Rumors of admittance constraints at the borders of the states were circulating even when people were travelling between states. For example, in May, the government of Uttar Pradesh prohibited the entry of buses from Rajasthan and Haryana. Karnataka barred entry to people from Gujarat, Maharashtra, and Tamil Nadu. As a consequence, travellers suffered as a result of restrictions on interstate travel after lockdowns. Neither the need nor the role of the Centre in fostering state-to-state cooperation at the grassroots level can be overstated.[31] The govt. of Assam said that the state of Rajasthan was responsible for the upsurge of COVID-19 cases in Assam. On May 6, 2020 a bus carrying 43 people from Rajasthan's "Ajmer Sharif", a "red zone," came back to Assam with 5 new cases.[32]

Although the state of West Bengal promised to do everything possible to get the tens of thousands of migrant workers who have been trapped throughout the nation back home, the State did nothing for implementation of its promise. It took the state to open its borders despite of contradictory orders for better support.[33] Increased numbers of Bengali employees in Maharashtra and Karnataka had taken on streets to express their displeasure at the state's refusal to let trains to transport them home. The eastern state of Bengal, according to the Gujarat administration, has refused to let migrant trains pass through. Jharkhand bus services were ordered back to the state's border with Bengal since there were no established procedures for operating the vehicles. State officials went to the federal government for help after Karnataka locked down its border, preventing essential food and medical supplies from reaching North Kerala.[34] As a result of the migrant workers' transportation costs, there was conflict among the States. Migrants who were sent to Muzaffarpur on a special train from Delhi were demanding payment from their home state. Delhi demanded a reimbursement from the Bihar government for bulk ticket purchases made for returning migrants. After their return to home, migrants were promised to be reimbursed for their rail cost at quarantine centres.[35]

Major Opposition-led states namely Maharashtra and Punjab were unable to meet their basic humanitarian commitments during this crisis and asked the Centre to expedite federal government payments." Due to a lack of money from the GST, several States were forced into financial hardship. There are some who question the centralization of the Canter's motives culminating in the ToRs[36] of the FC[37], where the FC was asked to examine whether revenue deficit grants should be provided to the State governments at all (ToR 5) and to recommend measures to control "populist measures by the States" (ToR 7 (viii) Besides forcing the FC to go beyond its constitutional role, these directives illustrate how non-elected authorities are being abused to restrict the budgetary space of States. Cooperative federalism and fiscal federalism are at odds with one other, and this undermines the basis of both.[38]

Even though the Covid-19 lockdown began to weaken its hold on the states, the initial top-down method limited their ability to formulate their own policies. A policy allowing corporate social responsibility donations to disaster management funds was implemented early on in the pandemic, for example. It was a privilege not accorded to the United States.

4.4.5 The Futuristic Purview of India's Federalism

As per the above overview and previous discussions, there was both collaboration and confrontation between state & federal govt. After the first lockdown, the federal govt. efforts to develop collaboration with the states diminished the probability of political conflict and policy ambiguity. However, cooperative federalism was undercut by the Central Govt. post-lockdown policies, including GST payment, agriculture laws, and Finance Commission's Terms of Reference. States governed by the opposition were clearly uncomfortable with these policies, as seen by their spats with the federal government. Many academics have questioned if federalism is even possible in the wake of the COVID-19 outbreak. Though not on equal footing, state governments headed by the NDA have been working closely with the central government to address threats posed by a coronavirus pandemic. GST was formerly hailed as a model of cooperative federalism, but it has been tarnished by the Centre's refusal to include the States in the distribution of GST revenues and by denying the States their due. An alarming trend for Indian federalism is that the GST Council's capacity to handle conflicts between the Centre and States has been called into question. An excellent example of Indian federal institution-building, the Council was hailed as a paradigm that should be reproduced in other policymaking verticals that need cooperation.[39]

When a pandemic like Covid-19 strikes, it is critical that the government's connection with its citizens be solid, trustworthy, and organic. In a centralised system of government, this will not be practicable. Local governments, with the help of the community, will play a key role in this,[40] The "73rd & 74th Constitutional Amendments, 1992" granted the Indian people local governments, the "gramme sabha," and other participation institutions; COVID-19 has helped them understand the significance and necessity of these institutions. These changes have made it possible for local governments like panchayats and municipalities to support social justice and economic progress. It was discovered in a recent research by Acharya and Porwal that in spite of all the government efforts, instances of the illness were documented in 627 of 640 districts (98 percent) in India. They stressed the importance of a tool for planning and setting priorities at the district level and for making the best use of resources.[41]

Local governments in Odisha, Rajasthan, and Kerala, three Indian states, play an important role in coordinating the pandemic response. This is due to the fact that they attempt to bridge the gap between the requirement for an immediate, forceful response to the pandemic and the local situation. It was discovered through interviews with middle and lower-level bureaucrats as well as an examination of policy documents just how quickly the COVID-19 response spawned new kinds of links across sectors and scales amongst administrative units connected with coordination. This is because local authorities took on a lot of responsibility for putting disease control as well as social security systems into place. Covid-19's problems couldn't be remedied without the cooperation of the States, the Centre recognized slowly. Frequent teleconferences between the PM and other senior ministers served as proof of this. Cooperative federalism was exhibited by the states' recognition that they needed guidance from the federal government to meet the pandemic's concerns, and the states' acknowledgment of the necessity to collaborate with the federal government. Central leaders must understand the adage "the more states that are well-governed, the less difficult it is for the nation as a whole" to understand. According to Varshney, this paradox, which claims that a strong centre necessitates weak states, is nonsensical.[42]

4.5 Conclusion

In addition to the COVID-19 pandemic, the economic slowdown, migrant labour dilemma, and China's threat to Indian Territory in Ladakh, India is engaged in a battle on several fronts. If there is a breakdown in confidence and collaboration between the federal government and the states, these challenges could be compounded. Cooperative federalism is therefore the only option that can be considered. According to what has already been said, recent history has seen the Centre & States work together as well as clash. As a result of the lengthy lockdown and COVID-19 pandemic, there has been a need for extraordinary collaboration and coordination across the States. Existing institutional institutions such as the ISC, which has mostly been dormant, urgently need revitalization. As a result of the pandemic, there were a number of issues that the ISC might have worked with states to resolve. During the nationwide lockdown, disputes occurred between the federal authority and each of the states. Despite this, subsequent efforts to strengthen coordination between state & federal govt. and the various areas of the nation decreased the possibility of political discord and policy misunderstanding. The states should be consulted on a regular basis, and they should be treated as equal participants in the federal system. There is no better time than now for the federal government to fulfil its promises to the states on the implementation of the GST. This pandemic might have been dealt with better had the Centre enabled States to make lockdown choices, as several analysts have remarked in their reports on the situation. In order for the pandemic to be dealt with head-on, both the federal and state governments must put politics aside. India's capacity to combat the COVID-19 pandemic is heavily reliant on the country's ability to handle both vertical and horizontal intergovernmental ties. As one of three layers of the federal framework, local government must be treated equally under India's future cooperative federalism.

Footnotes

1 AIR 1978 SC 68.

2 Oommen- "Covid-19 in the Indian context and the quest for alternative paradigms", Economic and Political Weekly, 55(45), 18–21, 2020.

3 Saxena R.- "Federalism and the Covid-19 crisis: Centre–State apposite relations in pandemic federalism—India", F.O.F., 2020; Available at:- http://www.forumfed.org/wp-content/uploads/2020/04/IndiaCovid3.pdf.

4 Parab – "Covid-19: Washington Post praises Mumbai's Dharavi efforts ", Deccan Chronicle, 2020.

5 W.H.O.- "*How India scaled up its laboratory testing capacity for Covid-19*", 2020, Available at https://www.who.int/india/news/feature-stories/detail/how-india-scaled-up-its-laboratory-testing-capacity-for-Covid19.

6 Supra Note 19.

7 Sarthak Sethi, "*Covid-19 and Indian Federalism: Through the Lens of the Disaster Management Act, 2005 and Fiscal Federalism*", *I.L.J.*

8 On March 24 (the initial shutdown) and April 15 (the extended lockdown), the Central Government issued a series of rag-bag executive orders covering a wide range of subjects that come within the purview of the State (7th Schedule of the Constitution). Government offices (Entry 41), including the state's hospitals (Entry 6), stores and marketplaces (Entry 28), industries (Entry 24), agriculture (Entry 14), and so on.

9 Supra Note 24.

10 Suhasini Raj, Jeffrey Gettleman, Sameer Yasir & Karan Deep Singh, "*The virus trains: How unplanned lockdown chaos spread Covid-19 across India* "*Business Standard*, 2020, Available at:- https://www.business-standard.com/article/current-affairs/the-virus-trains-how-unplanned-lockdown-chaos-spread-covid-19-across-india-120121600103_1.html.

11 Amrita Madhukalya- *"Covid-19: States protest against Centre's directive on PPE procurement"*, H.T.,2020, Available at- https://www.hindustantimes.com/india-news/covid-19-states-protest-against-centre-s-directive-on-ppe-procurement/story-C2HLEkLKvPL9gMYGA494LP.html.

12 Ibid.

13 Anirudh Burman- "*How Covid-19 is changing Indian federalism", Carnegie India,July 28, 2020, How COVID-19 is Changing Indian Federalism",* Carnegie India, 2020.

14 Anubhav Khamroi- *"Federalism and Covid-19: Analysing the National Importance of Justification of the Centre*", *L.S.P.R., 2020.*

15 COVID-19, given its pan-India nature, saw a centralised and fast coordinated reaction headed by the federal government with its customary arbitrariness during lockdown periods, but such a response was difficult to continue in the latter phases of the pandemic. A decentralised response was necessary in order to handle the pandemic's dynamic character and scope, which needed governments to play an important role. It was clear even during the lockdown that a hyper-centralised approach had its limits, and the Center was quick to acknowledge the crucial roles played by states and local governments in putting an effective response in place. States were granted back control over lockdown measures, essential rules, and containment zoning after the federal government decided to take an advising role in several crucial decisions.[47] The Center for Disease Control and Prevention was impressed by the efficiency with which states like Delhi and Kerala dealt with the issue at various stages of the epidemic.

16 Ibid.

17 Nikunj Ohri-*"Centre Still Owes States Over Rs 30,000 Crore In GST Dues For FY20"*,Quint, 2020.

18 Ibid.

19 Hassan M Kamal- "*Kumbh Mela and election rallies: How two super spreader events have contributed to India's massive second wave of COVID-19 cases"*, 2021.

20 Ibid.

21 Varinder Bhatia & Mallika Joshi- "Oxygen Politics between Delhi, Haryana and UP", I.E., 2021.

22 Chandrakant Lahariya- "Covid vaccination was always Centre's Job, what else must be done",*The Quint*, 2021.

23 Partha Mukhopadhyay- "Forget play, the machine needs to be scrapped",*T.H.*, 2021.

24 As the number of cases increased, several state governments complained loudly about the Center's slowness, but it turned out that they had been slow to assess the situation on the ground in their states, alert the Center of the danger, and apply pressure for vaccinations early in the process.

25 No Fourth Wave of Coronavirus will Occue in India - Virologist Jacob John - Available athttps://www.google.com/amp/s/m.economictimes.com/news/india/no-fourth-wave-of-coronavirus-will-occur-in-india-virologist-t-jacob-john/amp_articleshow/90073003.cms (Last accessed on 22nd June 2022, 4:30 pm)

26 Ibid.

27 Supra note 24.

28 Ghosh, J. –"A critique of the Indian government's response to the Covid-19 pandemic" I.B.E.J., 47, 519–530, 2020.

29 Beg- "Centre should consult states regularly, treat them as equal partners: Rajasthan CM Ashok Gehlot on fight against Covid-19", Outlook, 2020.

30 Kumar- "Lockdown will fail if migrants return by bus", Deccan Herald, 2020.

31 Agarwal R.- "Achieving coordinated action through inter-state council" L.S.P.R., 2020, https://lawschoolpolicyreview.com/2020/08/08/achieving-coordinated-action-through-inter-state-cooperation/.

32 Kalita, P. – "*Coronavirus: Ajmer Sharif returnees new worry for Assam govt*" T.O.I., 2020.

33 Sharma, R., Ghosh, S., Mitra A & Bhattacharya, R.- "*Code Red: The uphill struggle in Gujarat and Bengal with country's highest Covid-19 case mortality*", I.E., 2020.

34 Smitha, T. K.- "SC directs union health secy to Resolve K'Taka –Kerala border issue" The Quaint, 2020.

35 Chakravarty, I.–"As lakhs of migrant workers try to go home, Indian states spar over logistics: The Centre, meanwhile, has gone missing", 2020, Available at:- https://scroll.in/article/961566/as-lakhs-of-migrant-workers-try-to-go-home-indian-states-spar-over-logistics.

36 Terms of Reference.

37 Finance Commission.

38 Ibid.

39 Chokkakula- "India's response to Covid-19 reflects the power, problems, potential of federalism ", I.E., 2020.

40 Ibid.

41 Porwal and Acharya- "A vulnerability index for the management of and response to the Covid-19 epidemic in India: An ecological study", L.G.H., 8(9), 2020.

42 Varshney- "*How has Indian federalism done? Studies in Indian Politics*", 1(1), 43–63, 2013.

05
CHAPTER

CONCLUSIONS AND SUGGESTIONS

5.1 Conclusion

Since its discovery in China in the latter half of 2019, and subsequent spread to other nations in the early beginning of 2020, research experts from all over the world have been examining the newly discovered virus. Governments, specialists, and the general public were all obliged to rely on dubious knowledge and experience earned through work in the appropriate field to confront this unprecedented and mostly unknown threat. Asian nations were alerted by rumors originating in China, and they responded swiftly by implementing a proactive eradication policy. This was done in light of the region's previous tragic experiences, such as the outbreak of SARS in 2003. When it came to the response of the WHO and other organizations in the Global North, it may be described as a lethargic and cautious one. They emphasized the necessity of being attentive, but they didn't take many precautionary measures. The Western world is reluctant to follow the cautious approach for a number of reasons, one of which is cultural symbolism. The widely extensive belief is that - the way of life and practices of the people of Asia, in particular China, are a source of infectious diseases. As a direct consequence of this, the industrialized nations of the West centered their policy on preventing the further spread of the virus and providing protection for those who were already afflicted. Nations who were in desperate need but lack amenities and aid received assistance from the WHO in the form of technology, finance, etc.

There was a common belief that COVID-19 might be contained inside the highly developed healthcare systems of the streamlined nations because they were believed to be prepared and had sufficient time to act like they did during MERS, SARS, and Ebola. Each of these three big outbreaks in the Middle East and Africa was effectively contained and handled within this established international division of labour that the whole world community supported.

Experts in socio-cultural trends were also able to provide data for political decision-making. The Western discussion over whether or not facemasks should be worn in public illustrates how culturally mediated behaviors and values are negotiated. People are better protected from illness when wearing facemasks, but health officials have revised their recommendations because of the transition from individual to public health. When everyone in a public place is wearing a facemask, there is minimal evidence that the mask can protect a person for an extended period of time. While the use of facemasks as a preventative measure against infectious illnesses is popular in many Asian nations, it was viewed with suspicion in the west where it was seen as a cultural quirk with no scientific proof to back up its effectiveness against disease outbreaks.[1] As a result, the WHO did not gave a green signal for approval before the end of March 2020[2] and many other nations in the Global North did not either.

Throughout the crises, science was critical in establishing the authority and legitimacy over political authorities.[3] Scientists and doctors are more reliable sources of information than politicians. When announcing their intentions to battle the epidemic, politicians frequently sought the counsel of medical experts. Strong leadership, as shown in New Zealand, made this approach extremely effective[4]. However, because science lacks a political compass and credibility, it is unable to serve as a decision-making authority in politics. It is necessary to consider the risks and benefits of various options and to be willing to accept a higher-than-expected death toll in order to choose between extermination and flattening the curve. Science alone cannot be relied upon to make decisions of this size. As a result, politicians were called out when they were caught offloading or trying to cover up political judgments with scientific information.[5] To put it another way, successful pandemic management necessitates excellent research, but political leadership is required to ensure the credibility of the findings.[6]

There were several ways in which worldwide societal disparities influenced the pandemic's reaction. Many democratic democracies in Europe's early days grappled with issues of privacy and civil liberties limits. In contrast to several govts. in the Global North, China, as well as other Asian countries, were far tighter in limiting travel during the early stages of the Pandemic. As a result, the use of technology methods to control the epidemic that had been effectively deployed elsewhere was restricted because of a rejection of automated monitoring as a danger to democracy and individual freedom. This presents issues with the development of technologically superior applications and also the costs and complexity of executing effective contact tracing on a large scale without the support of efficient technology. There is a possibility that new solutions can be developed to meet the requirements of pandemic control as well as data security.[7]

Governments used a variety of methods when cultural values were in jeopardy. Lunar New Year festivities in China and Iran were cancelled in January 2020 due to fatal virus worries, and numerous megacities were placed under lockdown. Iran began cancelling public activities in February but didn't close the Shia sites in Qom until mid-March. Over religious objections to effective pandemic management, several European governments were inclined to decrease critical safeguards. A reversal in pandemic control was observed in early 2021 when the German government loosened its restriction on face-to-face contact during the Christmas season to allow families to celebrate together. During the 2nd wave of the disease outbreak in 2021, India let a large Hindu celebration occur in the Ganges River. This caused a super-spreader event and put too much stress on the healthcare system.[8]

There are a number of concerns that need to be addressed in various ways, such as the growth in domestic violence. Some 30 to 50 percent of those in nursing and retirement facilities perished, while the poor in many nations were disproportionately affected for a variety of causes (such as living conditions, language, health).[9] A lack of attention to marginalised groups meant that they were usually ignored. The risk of death and infection from COVID-19 remained strongly correlated with a wide range of socio-structural variables. Socio-cultural, institutional, and deeply ingrained socio-structural factors affected global and national reactions to the crisis. Othering & stigma, loyalty, daily risk rationalities and risk communication are just a few of the issues addressed in this monograph edition of the Journal of Risk Research. While socio-cultural factors impacted politicians and the general public, these factors also influenced concrete actions and arguments. However, governments responded differently to various concerns because the pandemic threat was sensed and manifested in diverse ways on a global scale. Now that the virus has been eradicated, different nation's main focus is on avoiding the spread of new cases. In countries where the rate of infection has risen out of control, those attempting to "flatten the curve" are experimenting with various behavioural techniques to stabilize an already congested healthcare system.

IHR[10] signatory India, however, has a number of deficiencies in its domestic legislation that need to be addressed. Art. 43 of the IHR states that limitations on commercial flights must be commensurate to the risk they pose. For instance, a nationwide ban on commercial planes may not be acceptable with Art. 43. Similarly, the necessity to disclose health information and the right of patients to privacy should be balanced. Researcher agree that there is nothing like this in the existing rules to keep this balance. A constitution could also include plans for an emergency savings to cope up with these kinds of problems. The IPC deals with crimes that affect health of public, safety, accessibility, moral integrity, and ethics. It is split into two main sections: one deals with "public nuisance", and the other deals with the "quarantine law". The EDA is an addition to the IPC law. The notion of quarantine is based on the concept of social isolation. India's stated position amid COVID-19 is the outcome of Sec. 6(2)(1) & 10(2)(1) of the DMA, which govern "quarantine law enforcement" as well as "health protection". Because such a statute did not exist in England at the time, the IPC was considered a visionary piece of legislation. The quarantine clause of the IPC is a vital component of the control of public nuisances in the workplace. Sec. 188, 269, 270, & 271 of the IPC, as well as Sec. 133 of Criminal Procedure Court (CrPC) are crucial in light of the current COVID-19 outbreak and nationwide lockdown restrictions. Sec. 269 of IPC says that "knowingly" doing something that is capable of spreading a virus of a disease that is dangerous to human health is subject to punishment by 6 months in jail, a penalty, or both. Section 270 of the penal code provides that any conduct likely to transmit a life-threatening disease or illness is punishable by a two-year prison sentence. Additionally, Section

271 states that violating quarantine laws is punishable by up to six months in prison or a fine of up to Rs.10,000. Art. 47 says that it is the state's main job to make sure people have enough food, raise their standard of living, and improve their general well-being.

5.1.1 Amicable relationship between Nature, Technology and Humans

It has been shown that society, nature, and technology interact in complicated ways because of the coronavirus problem, and material semiotics have stressed this importance. COVID-19 offers an excellent opportunity to learn about the intricate relationships that exist between various types of organisms and their surroundings, including modern technology. History shows us that this reality varied and altered perceptions throughout time by looking back at discussions over whether or not the virus existed. In particular, several nations used their geographic advantage in border control to benefit from an effective viral extermination approach. Social constructs, such as the facemask, are an example of this, as are discussions about the shifting focus from individual protection to population safety in response to changing social conditions. It was also a chance to examine the relationship between people and nature and the role of technology as the epidemic unfolded. It is the responsibility of those afflicted to put a halt on harm to the environment and to ensure that the required resources are available to combat the virus.[11]

During the 2003 SARS pandemic, doctors in Wuhan began treating patients with symptoms similar to those seen in SARS patients. Despite the lack of scientific evidence, a doctor working at a hospital brought up the subject of their fears. Authorities held off on disclosing the existence of a new coronavirus until they had a chance to isolate it in the lab. Formal scientific validation was required even in cases where human-to-human transmission was suspected to assess the scope of the problem. One theory being floated is that China's government may have tried to cover up the outbreak, as some analysts have suggested. However, there is a much deeper problem at hand." Every new danger necessitates a fine line between exaggeration and reductionism.[12] The capacity to cite to a corpus of scientific evidence in order to deflect responsibility is increasingly valuable in today's world of growing accountability. Delaying action until additional research has been done, on the other hand, raises the likelihood of negative outcomes. Excellent risk management relies on soft sorts of experience-based knowledge, such as intuition. A lot of this is based on 'well-informed supposition,' rather than on actual facts.

Additionally, there were outstanding examples of how social variables can influence scientific information creation while showing how scientific and practical knowledge management can coexist well. First cases of infection in a Bavarian company were studied to discover if the virus could spread without causing any symptoms. Since the researchers couldn't talk to the person who made the virus, they had to rely on what the people in the study said. They said the Chinese tourist didn't seem to have any obvious health problems. As a result, the online pre-published research was deemed unscientific because it had not spoken to a real patient. Instead of squabbling over who might claim to be the greatest, we should work to define what it means to be "socially asymptomatic". A translation and explanation of scientific facts into people's everyday comprehension, which has its own criteria and prerequisites for illness, is essential. Swellings, aches, pains, and other symptoms are not worthy of further inquiry in the scientific sense. It is impossible to separate symptoms from their social and cultural surroundings. Our focus here is on how separate physical realities are conceptualised for this investigation. There is a similar issue in the argument about face masks.

The facemask debate demonstrates that evidence-based recommendations are subject to a number of influences. As a starting point, the caretakers didn't have enough facemasks. The appropriateness of facemasks as a means of protecting either the wearer or the general public was also called into question. When it comes to this issue, material semiotics indicates that it wasn't about cultural differences or different perspectives on the same reality. The strategy's change from defending individuals to safeguarding the population was validated by other evidence.

Society-nature-technology "Nexus" might also help us figure out what happens when a virus spreads quickly from hotspots or "mega spreading" events. When the conditions are right, like when there are many people and things to do in a dance club and a soccer stadium, the infection spreads quickly. For example- A prominent Austrian ski resort has been linked to hundreds of instances of the virus in six European nations, as have the highly mobile individuals who congregated there, such as in Ischgl. There were even hints that the virus originated from a certain pub in Ischgl and that certain habits like playing oral beer pong and exchanging whistles made it easy for the infection to spread by saliva interchange. On 19th Feb. 2020, a soccer game in Milan between Valencia (Spain) as well as Atalante (Italy) was called a "super-spreader" because it was thought to have sped up the disease transmission in both Italy & Spain. Other incidents like these spread a local virus over the world. This is due to the fact that modern technology makes it easy for people to spread the virus when they travel and return home. The way people greet each other (kissing on both cheeks, shaking hands, etc.) is one instance of a cultural norm that COVID-19 tested because it has become annoying and is being looked into as a possible cause of contamination.

5.1.2 Zero Coordination

We cannot comprehend the issue without considering the rapid digitalization and digital divides that have emerged in recent years. Throughout the pandemic, social media and social digitization played a significant role in people's experiences and responses. Lockdown crisis management relies heavily on social media, which is often seen as an unreliable source of information. It is true that social media has played a significant part in giving essential information, keeping people in touch with loved ones, or keeping students motivated with their studies to offer meaning and purpose to life in confinement. Under lockdown, they experimented with and devised new methods to utilize digital media (such as video conferencing to observe the same show simultaneously). To keep their social interactions continuing when physical contact was prohibited or not feasible, they used a survival technique that has become an essential resource in their life or that they may fall back on in the event of another crisis. Owing to the lengthy lockdown, people created distance requirements for face-to-face contacts, but everyone desired to catch up with friends and relatives in person. Others re-evaluated the social pressure some young adults had previously been under, and some discovered they preferred having more time to do their own thing. As a result, social media may help people find new ways to incorporate digital media into their daily lives to resist social pressures they don't want. Is it possible to better manage the depth and commitments of friendships by socializing online, or is this just a way to better restrict connections? It's becoming possible for individuals to participate in a wide range of activities over the Internet, from virtual visits to museums and cities to online sports training sessions with coaches from across the world. To put it another way, the concept of 'digital health' may shift because it refers to utilizing the expanded digital world or the virtual world for mental and physical health.

Researchers have established a link between an increase in the number of zoonotic illnesses and environmental degradation, including a decline in biodiversity, which the society-nature-technology nexus points to as natural ecosystems are destroyed and human interaction with wild animals carrying a range of illnesses increases, there is an increased risk of viruses crossing species borders. This aligns with the "One World, One Health" concept. We are just now starting to appreciate how helpful bacteria and viruses may be, not only for digestion & health but also on the skin as well as in our surroundings. The "One World, One Health" strategy might benefit from incorporating a social viewpoint into its emphasis on disease transmission.

Understanding the dynamics of the coronavirus problem requires considering the intersection of society, nature, and technology. Both the health care institutions and society as a whole must be able to handle appropriate actions such as lockdowns, contact tracking, and compliance enforcement if this is to be accomplished. There is no substitute for face-to-face interaction, but digital media may aid for a short period of time to keep up-to-date, connect, and give emotional support.

A "new normal" following the coronavirus may be useless when most individuals are yearning to return to their "regular" lives. Even though India was in the midst of a terrible outbreak with no sufficient vaccines, oxygen or intensive care beds, it is unknown to what extent various nations' vaccination programmes will be adequate to exterminate the virus. Hand cleaning, social distance, contact tracing, and lockdowns may be necessary even if most individuals are vaccinated since the virus may persist for some time. We don't know enough about COVID-19 to anticipate how it will behave in the future or which mutations will arise in hotspots around the world.

No matter how this pandemic develops, it is important to include social factors in building technical and political instruments for acceptable responses. As our natural environment deteriorates, the prevalence of zoonotic diseases increases. A deeper understanding of how contemporary subjectivities impact people's perceptions, comprehension, and responses may be useful in the event of future pandemics. Theses can differ considerably based on how people are directly affected (for example, if a family member dies or if they get sick), how they live (for example, if they have a lot of money or a certain way of life), and how they are divided across borders. While generalizations remain difficult, certain reflections may be beneficial while being aware of their restricted application.

COVID-19 impact on people's broad awareness of viruses, epidemics, and essential actions is one of the most critical problems for future pandemics. In the face of restrictions like curfews or self-imposed isolation, people will still need to labour to meet their basic requirements and rely on other social components to do so. This list doesn't include important things like washing hands and wearing face masks. We have all the proof that a person is more likely to change their behaviour when specific events in their own lives back it up. Strong, highly emotional memories of the epidemic may impact people's behaviour in the future if they have been directly afflicted by COVID-19 or have contaminated a family member or friend.

In the future, it will be fascinating to see if people's perceptions of nature shift from seeing it as a disease-free sanctuary to perceive it as an ecosystem full of risks and needs continuous care. In addition to the direct dangers posed by man-made dangers (such as contaminated sites), the natural and social environments can pose indirect dangers that could change long-term attitudes and behaviours.

COVID-19 was a wake-up call to the wealthy and elderly nations of the Global North that they are susceptible to viruses that were previously isolated elsewhere. Wild animal viruses and nature are becoming more intertwined, raising the possibility of a pandemic and necessitating international cooperation. According to Ulrich Beck, a German sociologist, the pandemic presents an opportunity for cosmopolitanism to expand. We do not yet know how much possibility global learning presents. Still, pandemics will cause long-term changes in how people think and act about the environment, and the way technology has changed the world.

5.1.3 Why Indian Strategies failed?

It is pertinent to mention that the Indian Government adopted the strategy of various countries and imposed all of the implications under one roof. From the timeline of India's covid-19 combat, it can be seen that it had approached various strategies as described above. It is seen from the governmental strategies that, at first, India imposed a nationwide lockdown across the whole country, which stopped all the daily lives and chores of the people at once without any secondary warning. Everyone was instructed to remain in their current cities and prohibited from returning to their hometown. However, this nationwide lockout lasted only two months, and the unlocking procedure began in June with minimal impact on transportation. From June onwards, a slow and steady unlock process had been one of the strategies of the Indian government.[13] But to everyone's surprise, India failed at restricting Covid cases and slowly by the end of 2020, India became the second highest country to deal with Covid-19 cases and Covid related deaths[14]. The question as to why India failed at following the Covid protocol has its answers hidden inside the factual variants and the cultural characteristics therein.

1. One of the main reasons as to why India failed at following a strong Covid protocol is to provide for lockdowns as the only strategy. While China, France and other Western and Asian countries essentially imposed several other restrictions, health facility and social activity such as *social distancing rule,* India did not impose any of those. It is true that India had tried to impose such strict restrictions of social distancing and many other rapid test facilities in many states but due to the rural factor of Indian governments, the lack of education among the citizens essentially became the biggest obstacles. Almost 95% of the Indian workers, working in different states of India are informal and thus the employers of such workers were not entitled to provide the employees with any kind of benefits during the lockdown situation which eventually created the severe situation of *migrant workers*[15].

2. Another main reason behind the failure is the centralisation of the legal powers. The Union Government essentially invoked and imposed the DMA of 2005 which only allowed the Central Govt. with the sole power and responsibility to handle COVID-19 situation. The lack of delegation of power from Central to State government essentially created chaos and as such the Central Government became overburdened.

3. When countries were put on lockdown, it was not only done to reduce the number of Covid-19 infections; it was done so that government officials could better comprehend the virus's severity and devise a second strategy for responding. So, once the lockdown is over, the govt. was supposed to come up with new and better standards and measures to cope up with the problem at Covid-19. Among many other things, the following are some of the most important things a govt. should do to fight Covid-19 are: increasing the size of the public health facilities and establish better health infrastructure and deploy public health force. Also, lockdown is the time to provide the authorities with the time to come up with better quarantine system and better health care plan for the affected persons. However, the same was not the case with India. The Central government essentially failed at doing the needful during the time of the lockdown. The efforts made by the State and the Central government only made it tougher for people to commute and understand the seriousness of this virus. The funds provided by the Central govt. with an aim to meet the needs of the public health sector were reported to spend only a meagre portion of the GDP only. Hence, apart from some of the states of India such as Kerala, none of the states of India dealt with Covid-19 in a smarter way and lockdown became essentially ineffective. It took about 2 months for the government to conduct rapid testing or more increasing rate of testing in different areas of India. In the month of July, 2020, the rate of testing essentially grew to 5371 testing per million but the same was moderately low rating. Basic supplies, like PPP for healthcare personnel, were not set up in a reasonable timeframe. As the prevalence of the symptoms grew, these items quickly ran out. Other facilities, like hospital beds, respirators, and so forth, were also in short supply compared to the number of people who needed them[16].

5.1.4 Analysis as to the Hypothesis of present thesis

H1: Indian public health legislation has a plethora of legislative rules, regulations, administrative orders, and notifications having a bearing on the various facets of public health dimensions and they are enough to provide an amicable solution to the COVID epidemic-pandemic situation.

When faced with pandemic COVID-19, the government tried its best to fulfil its constitutional commitment to adopt public health and disaster preparation regulations in India. The "Epidemic Diseases Act, 1897", or, at best, "the Disaster Management Act, 2005", served as a cover for it. Under the "International Health Regulations, 2005", a lot of changes were made to the laws dealing with biological, chemical, as well as radioactive risks at the entrance, control and remediation levels. The "National Health Bill of 2009" and the "Health Personnel and Clinical Establishments (Prohibition of Violence and Damage to Property) Bill of 2019" are as of now in predicament. A significant step forward in public healthcare was taken with the passage of the 2009 National Health Bill, which addressed the human rights component of the issue. Excessive incidences of illness in a certain time period, as well as any reference to disease outbreaks, were described as epidemics in the law. Governments had to guarantee that the right to excellent health care and the well-being of everyone was given equal priority as well as adequate steps to prevent, cure, and control epidemics and endemic illnesses. Though Essential Commodities act along with its amendment and other acts have been successful in fulfilling the present demands of public, same have been found to be insufficient in case of future unseen calamities. As a result of the issue, an opportunity arose to address long-standing reforms in public health regulations, but this chance was blown. These laws, rules and efforts are all significant in the contemporary issue, but they do not solve various the ethical problems of faced while dealing the issue. For said problems the old acts and legislative imperatives were found to be insufficient, hence it is disproved.

H2: The quarantine regulation established under the 160-year-old IPC of 1860 and the 123-year-old EDA of 1897 proved efficient in managing the dreadful COVID-19 pandemic.

For Central and State governments to make emergency notifications and provide almost limitless authority in the event of an infectious and deadly epidemic, the Epidemic Diseases Act, 1897, the Amendment Bill, 2020 and IPC, 1860 offer a framework when read together. However, in practice, these abilities do not guarantee a synergistic and successful reaction. Action plans are needed in India to identify an outbreak situation and quickly gather data regarding the same, isolate critical infected regions on a grid basis, collaborate with authorities at various levels, ensure the continued supply of essential services and safety kits, ensure sanitation to control the spread of communicable diseases, and share information about effective models for combating the spread of the disease in question. These laws outline the first steps to be taken in the event that a local outbreak occurs and / or a resurgence of the disease, such as public notification, the distribution of funds, and compensation packages. Safe migration protocols and ongoing surveillance of illness trends should be implemented as well. The Amendment Bill proved to be a short-term solution; hence it is proved.

H3: The nationwide lockdowns imposed under Sec. 6, 10, 38, & 72 of the DMA of 2005 aided much in coping with the tremendous issues of COVID-19.

The sheer size of India's population made coping with calamities, particularly pandemics like COVID-19, a logistical nightmare. But still, overall management, on the other hand, was reinforced in three different ways which turned out to be successful despite of such a huge number of populations. In the first place, a national-scale biological crisis required a coordinated response from the federal government and state govts., disaster management agencies, and other stakeholders, which was well implemented. All levels of government, including federal, state, and local, worked cooperatively and consultatively in keeping with the spirit of the DMA and the federal system. Millions of people in the nation were directly affected by issues such as migratory labour migration, food availability, securing livelihoods for daily wagers, relief camps, and the right to statutory minimum relief. Hence, the DMA was found to be conducive in carrying out the responsibilities as far as lockdown, and its implementation were concerned, therefore it is proved.

H4: The PH (Prevention, Control and Management of Epidemics, Bio-Terrorism and Disasters) Bill (was drafted in 2017) would have been the precise legislation to put into effect when COVID-19 struck.

The "Public Health (Prevention, Control and Management of Epidemics, Bioterrorism, and Catastrophes) Bill, 2017", which was recently brought to light. Authorities from the Union Ministry of Health and Family Welfare are making changes to different parts of the current draught of the Bill. The Bill will likely be presented to Parliament soon. If the Bill is passed, it will substitute the "Epidemic Diseases Act of 1897" In recent years, the law hasn't been changed, and there haven't been any new Rules or Regulations to back it up. For future performance, these are the things that the govt. has learned from their past experiences that must be put into practice correctly but old bill of 2017 might not be best solution as that there was no reference of COVID-19 but the newly amended bill might be., hence it is disproved.

5.2 Suggestions

Following the evaluation of various legislative and constitutional provisions, 3 components emerge from our research to improve India's legal and constitutional structures for dealing with COVID-19 and similar future events. To begin, there is an urgent need to assess colonial period EDA. Second, it is critical to adopt comprehensive law that covers all aspects of health & guarantees everyone the Right to health. Finally, there is a need to investigate alternative approaches to incorporating health emergency measures within the Indian Constitution. Here listing below enlarge suggestions-

A. **Amendments to EDA, 1897:** The EDA is imperfect on the following grounds.

   (1) The law fails to identify and categorise different types of illnesses, as well as their severity.

   (2) The statute does not address the confinement procedure or the establishment of zones based on risk categories; it merely demands that the state limit the subject's mobility.

   (3) The role of Panchayats as well as other local governments isn't addressed in the statute.

   (4) The Act completely ignores pharmaceutical and vaccination constraints during pandemic.

(5) The act emphasises restricting disease spread by ship, but it makes no mention of airline travel.

Given the current situation, wherein air travel considerably outnumbers marine travel, there is a compelling need for tougher screening processes to be established at airports and by airlines. The relevant modifications are necessary to improve:

(1) Improvements are needed to identify, test, isolate, trace, control, coordinate and restrict any outbreak in terms of making the EDA to combat any future health crisis.

(2) Modifications are necessary to include the definition & categorization of various ailments, as well as the demarcation of regions depending on levels of severity.

(3) Furthermore, it is imperative that the Union's function be clearly defined so that it can better collaborate with state and municipal govts.

(4) Legislation should handle and incorporate the development of quarantine facilities at or near airports. Identifying quarantine places that are both geographically and scientifically beneficial. These should be put in regions where there is a lower stream of people, such as in rural areas.

B. **Requirement for a national "Public Health Law":** The second approach is to pass centeral public health legistation. To reform India's public health regulations, it is necessary to examine legislation at the sub-national and international levels. A detailed national public health law should be formed at how other nations have respond to a health emergency and try to improve India's law whereas maintaining political, social, cultural, economic, as well as environmental issues in mind. The role of the Union is vital in establishing a climate for a comprehensive public health legislation by assessing and resolving the concerns of the states. According to reports, the Union government is now finalising and drafting a new National Public Health Bill that could be submitted during the Monsoon Session of Parliament. It's meant to take the place of the Epidemic Diseases Act of 1897. The Public Health (Prevention,

Control and Management of Epidemics, Bioterrorism and Disasters) Bill, which, although being made available for public deliberation in February 2017, was unable to pass. Even though the new Bill and its contents have not yet been formally announced, it is worthwhile to review those included in the previous version in light of the profound shift in public opinion brought on by the coronavirus pandemic.

The following provisions should be included in the comprehensive public health legislation in order to ensure that citizens have access to healthcare (in addition to already 2022 bill):

1. It should be evident what the state, union, as well as local govts. (Like municipalities & panchayats) are supposed to do.

2. It would be crucial to establish complementarity and prevent conflict among the sections of the possible The Public Health (Prevention, Control and Management of Epidemics, Bioterrorism and Disasters) Bill because many of them would end up overlapping with those of the Disaster Management Act, 2005.

    - The major focus will probably still be on epidemics. This would imply that it lives up to its name, yet being extremely wide in breadth is neither sensible nor prudent.
    - It's crucial to know where to draw the line, and while the new Bill should keep public health emergencies as its main priority, it should also always recognise the holistic character of emergency responses and widen its focus to include other closely linked issues.
    - There should be a social institution which can connect govts., research centers, as well as healthcare providers into a network.
    - In order to control epidemics in a timely and proper manner, the Act shall establish numerous tools and procedures for monitoring testing and treatment.
    - Fiscal & temporary aid for local and state governments during medical emergencies should be considered.

3. With the passage of this legislation, the Right to Health will be officially specified in the Indian Constitution, as well as provisions for expanding the country's medical infrastructure. Till than an amendment are required so current and immediate future problems can resolved.

4. People who work in healthcare and hygiene should get extra protection, taking into account how society works.

5. There is a major resource disparity between health institutions and the country's governing structure, as seen above. As a result, many have been compelled to pay far higher costs for essential prescriptions and gadgets; others are unable to do so at all, resulting to deaths that might have been prevented. While amending the Essential Commodities Act, here are some ideas the Central Government should explore. Under the act, all medical medications and equipment must be declared essential commodities. In addition, state governments have issued a number of notifications that classify medical pharmaceuticals as essential commodities, but do not yet include medical equipment. If the ECA's restrictions are changed, the illicit market for crucial medical goods will be lessened, perhaps saving lives.

   - The ECA's provisions may be enabled by the national government.
   - The Ministry of Corporate Affairs and Food Public Distribution announced on March 21, 2020 that the price of hand sanitizers and face masks will be fixed. Medical supply hoarding would decrease if the price of necessary medical supplies was restricted, and these services would be offered at a set fee to people from low-income families. More lives are saved when there is less scarcity.
   - Hoarding and black-marketing offences should not be subject to bail or compounding. Changes such as set pricing and criminalising hoarding, among other things, must be made under the ECA as soon as possible. Like - There is no defined price for the sale of other medical

equipment believed to be just as necessary, notwithstanding a government notice dated 25.09.2020 that set rates for liquid medical oxygen and oxygen inhalation minus GST should be made future also.

- Under Section 2A r/w Section 3 of the ECA, the central government should also issue an order to regulate prices. If an order for regulation is issued under Section 7 of the ECA Act, it can be utilised to penalise those who break the regulations.
- There should be fast-track courts that have the authority to handle such cases Medicinal products should be subject to the Essential Commodities Act's price controls.
- As a consequence of any violation, a person might face up to seven years in jail, as well as fines, property confiscation, and other punishments. Drugs and equipment seized by law enforcement might potentially be released this way.

C. The Indian Constitution includes provisions for health emergencies.

The Indian Constitution, as previously stated, contains no provisions for health emergencies. France enacted the Emergency Response to the COVID-19 Disease Act (2020) in a quick process on March 23, 2020, to contain and control the epidemic that was recently declared following the outbreak declaration. According to the new Act. L.3131 12 article of the French Constitution provides, "the State of health emergency may be proclaimed in the event of a health catastrophe jeopardizing, by its nature and seriousness, the health of the population". Japan similarly triggered a health emergency clause on April 7, 2020, by modifying the New Influenza Special Measures Act. Article 352 of the Indian Constitution authorizes the President to establish an emergency "whereby the security of India or any portion thereof is endangered whether by war or foreign attack or armed rebellion."

However, a health emergency is not grounds for creating a national emergency and limiting the movement of persons. India should study several alternatives for incorporating a health emergency clause into the Indian Constitution. Because emergency measures infringe on people's fundamental rights, there must be a public debate both inside and outside of Parliament.

D. **Fiscal and Co-operative Federalism of States need to be strengthened** wherein States need to be more compassionate with respect to the needs of their own region as well as other states. The way migrant workers and certain sects of citizens were treated during Pandemic has shown the failure on compassionate grounds, which has led to co-operative federalism being followed only at Centre-State Level but not among the states that unite and make the national integrity.

E. **Work or Study from home**

For many workers, the ability to work from home when high-speed Internet is available was made possible in part by the COVID-19 experience. It is conceivable that the distinction between work that needs physical presence and labour that does not necessitate physical presence would expand due to this trend toward working from home for particular vocations. Working in the unregulated labour market entails the additional weight of infection risk as well as the dangers of the pandemic reaction, such as the loss of income. Digital divides in schooling are also expected to rise. School districts and universities were able to transition to online teaching and training in the North's wealthier nations. This left people who couldn't afford decent working circumstances at home behind. Education was shut down in other nations for a long period of time, with no documented long-term impacts. The digital gap is expected to expand not just in terms of employment and education. Even in the face of the epidemic, digital media access is crucial for maintaining a social life. While not a replacement for face-to-face contact, it has proven to be an indispensable tool for staying informed, coordinating aid, and maintaining social relationships. The effects of organizing one's life around digital media may be double for this generation. Sharing physical activities with friends, while being more skilled at using electronic channels to organize social contacts is an important part of social networking. Developing these abilities may become increasingly important as work and school schedules become more adaptable.[17] Hence, a separate legislation should be design in order to meet this need.

Footnotes

1 Fleming A.- "Our face mask future: Do they really help beat flu, coronavirus and pollution? "2020.. Available at: www.theguardian.com/world/2020/jan/31/our-face-mask-future-do-they-really-help-beat-flu-coronavirus-and-pollution

2 Howard, J– "To help stop coronavirus, everyone should be wearing face masks." The Guardian, 2020. Available at: www.theguardian. com/commentisfree/2020/apr/04/why-wear-a-mask-may-be-our-best-weapon-to-stop-coronavirus

3 Balog-Way, DHP, McComas, KA– "COVID19: Reflections on trust, trade-offs, and preparedness", J.R.R., 2020.

4 Ibid.

5 Runciman D.- "Coronavirus has not suspended politics– it has revealed the nature of power", The Guardian, 2020. Available at: www.theguardian.com/commentisfree/2020/ mar/27/ coronavirus-politics-lockdown-hobbes

6 Ibid.

7 DW (2020)- "China cancels Lunar New Year events over deadly virus fears." 2020. Available at: www.dw.com/en/china-cancels-lunar-new-year-events-over-deadly-virus-fears/a-52121516

8 Ibid.

9 Booth R.– "BAME groups hit harder by Covid-19 than white people", 2020. The Guardian, 2020. Available at: www.theguardian.com/world/2020/apr/07/bame-groups-hit-hardercovid-19-than-white-people-uk

10 The Worldwide Health Regulations (IHR) (International Health Regulations) are a legislative document that governs international efforts to control the transmission of infectious illnesses across borders. The International Human Rights Convention (IHRC) was accepted by the 58th World Health Assembly in 2005 through Resolution WHA58.

11 Latour, B– "*Reassembling the Social: An Introduction to Actor-Network-Theory*",O.U.P., 1999.

12 Ibid.

13 Karotia D, Kumar A (2020). *A Perspective on India's Fight against COVID - 19*. Epidem Int; 5(1): 22-28.

14 *Supra*

15 Zodpey, S., Negandhi, H., Dua, A., Vasudevan, A., & Raja, M. (2020). *Our Fight Against the Rapidly Evolving COVID-19 Pandemic: A Review of India's Actions and Proposed Way Forward.* Indian journal of community medicine : official publication of Indian Association of Preventive & Social Medicine, 45(2), 117–124. https://doi.org/10.4103/ijcm.IJCM_221_20

16 Ibid

17 Kaufmann, K, Straganz, C, Bork-Hüffner, T– "City-life no more? Young adults' disrupted urban experiences and their digital mediation under Covid-19, U.P. 2020.

BIBLIOGRAPHY

Books

1. Craven M- The International Covenant on Economic, Social and Cultural Rights: A Perspective on Its Development. (Clanderon Press, 1995).
2. Garrison Fh – An Introduction to the History of Medicine along with Medical Chronology, (Saunders 1929).
3. Lamb G- The Etiology and Epidemiology of Plague. A Summary of the Work of the Plague Commission. Issued under the Authority of the Government of India, (2010).
4. Marnot M & Willinkson Rc- Social Determinants of Health (Oxford University Press, 1999).
5. Mark Harrison- Public Health in British India: Anglo Indian Preventive Medicine 1859-1914, (Cambridge University Press, 1994).
6. Nathan R- The Plague in India 1896-1897. (Government Central Print Office 1898).
7. Park K - Park's Textbook of Preventive and Social Medicine. " (Banarsidas Publishers, 2005).
8. Hannah Ritchie, Edouard Mathieu, Lucas Rodés-Guirao, Cameron Appel, Charlie Giattino, Esteban Ortiz-Ospina, Joe Hasell, Bobbie Macdonald, Diana Beltekian and Max Roser (2020) - "Coronavirus Pandemic (COVID-19)". OurWorldInData.org. (Last accessed on Oct, 12th, 2021).
9. Mishra, S., Scott, J.A., Laydon, D.J. et al - Comparing the responses of the UK, Sweden and Denmark to COVID-19 using counterfactual modelling. Sci Rep (2021).
10. Flaxman, S. et al - Estimating the effects of non-pharmaceutical interventions on COVID-19 in Europe. NATURE (2020).

11. Gelfand, M. J. -. Culture's constraints: International differences in the strength of social norms. P.S., (2012).
12. Markus, H., Kitayama, S. - Culture and the self: Implications for cognition, emotion, and motivation. P.R. (1991)
13. Kraemer, M. U. G., Yang, C.-H., Gutierrez, B., Wu, C.-H., Klein, B., Pigott, D. M., Scarpino, S. V. - The effect of human mobility and control measures on the COVID-19 epidemic in China. Science, (2020).
14. Zhang, S., et al - COVID-19 containment: China provides important lessons for global response. FRONTIERS (2020).
15. AlTakarli N.S. - China's Response to the COVID-19 Outbreak: A Model for Epidemic Preparedness and Management. D.M.J. (2020)
16. Burki, Talha - China's successful control of COVID-19. LANCET (2020).
17. AlTakarli N.S. - China's Response to the COVID-19 Outbreak: A Model for Epidemic Preparedness and Management. D.M.J. (2020).
18. Bradt, J. (2019). Comparing the effects of behaviorally informed interventions on flood insurance demand: An experimental analysis of "boosts" and "nudges." A.O.P. (2019).
19. Hayasaki, E. - Covid-19: How Japan squandered its early jump on the pandemic. BMJ (2020).
20. Jacobs, A. J.- Devolving authority and expanding autonomy in Japanese prefectures and municipalities. GOVERNANCE (2003).
21. Sunohara S, Asakura T, Kimura T, Ozawa S, Oshima S, Yamauchi D, et al.- Effective vaccine allocation strategies, balancing economy with infection control against COVID-19 in Japan. PLOS ONE (2021).
22. Shimizu K, Negita M - Lessons Learned from Japan's Response to the First Wave of COVID-19: A Content Analysis, (2021).
23. Ghosh, J. "A critique of the Indian government's response to the COVID-19 pandemic." J. IND. BUS ECON (2020)

24. M.Z.M Noman, Mohammad Rauf, Zubair Ahmed, Tarique Faiyaz, Saif A. Khan & Madiha Tahreem. "Quarantine Law Enforcement & Corona Virus (COVID-19) Pandemic in India" J.X.U. (2020).
25. Shamasunder, Sriram, et al. "COVID-19 reveals weak health systems by design: why we must re-make global health in this historic moment." G.P.H. (2020).
26. Pal, R., & Yadav, U. (2020). COVID-19 Pandemic in India: Present Scenario and a Steep Climb Ahead. Journal of primary care & community health, 11, 2150132720939402. https://doi.org/10.1177/2150132720939402

Journals and Articles

1. Bahn Ak and mausner J- "*Epidemiology- An introductory test*" P.I.T., (1974).
2. Bannerman WB.-" *Statistics of inoculations with Haffkine's anti-plague vaccine 1897-1900: Compiled from records in the Plague Department of the Secretariat and the Plague Research Laboratory, Bombay*" G.C.P., (1900).
3. Balog-Way, DHP, McComas, KA – "*COVID19: Reflections on trust, trade-offs, and preparedness*", J.R.R., (2020).
4. Baker, P – "*American and British English. Divided by a Common Language?*" C.U.P., (2017).
5. Bellew HW. – "*Cholera in India, 1862 to 1881: Bengal Province, 1862 to 1881, and review*", B.S.P., (1884).
6. Bentley CA.- "*Report of an investigation into the causes of malaria in Bombay and the measures necessary for its control*" G.C.P., (1911).
7. Bhadra, A., Mukherjee, A., & Sarkar, K. *Impact of population density on Covid-19 infected and mortality rate in India.* Modeling earth systems and environment, 1–7, A.O.P., (2020).
8. Burkle F. *Global Health security demands a strong international health regulations treaty and leadership from a highly resourced World Health Organization.* Disaster Med Public Health Prepared. (2015).

9. Claeson M, Hanson S - *COVID-19 and the Swedish enigma*. LANCET (2020).
10. Christensen, T., Lægreid, P., Rykkja, L. H. (2016). *Organizing for crisis management: Building governance capacity and legitimacy.* Public Administration Review, 76(6), 887–897.
11. Campbell JM, Mostyn R.- "*Report of the Bombay Plague Committee, appointed by government resolution no. 1204/ 720P, on the plague in Bombay, for the period extending from the 1st July 1897 to the 30th April 1898*" T.O.I., (1898).
12. Clemow F.- "*Pandemic of influenza*" 1, LANCET, (1894).
13. Cohen J.- *Here comes swine flu phase 6,* (2009).
14. Couchman ME- "*Account of plague administration in the Bombay Presidency from September 1896 till May 1897*", G.C.P., (1897).
15. Condon JK- "*The Bombay plague: being a history of the progress of plague in the Bombay presidency from September 1896 to June 1899_compiled under the orders of government*", B.E.S., (1900).
16. Cornish WR.- "*Cholera in southern India: A record of the progress of cholera in 1870, and resume of the records of former epidemic invasions of the Madras Presidency.*" G.G.P., (1871).
17. Christophers SR, Bentley CA.- "*Malaria in the Duars: Being the second report to the advisory committee appointed by the Government of India to conduct an enquiry regarding black water and other fevers prevalent in the Duars.*" G.M.P., (1911).
18. Fauci S, Morens DM and Taubenberger JK-*The persistent legacy of 1918 influenza virus,* 2., N.E.J.M., (2009).
19. Fischhoff, B – "*Risk perception and communicating unplugged: Twenty years of process*", RISK ANALYSIS (1995).
20. Gatacre WF-"*Report on the bubonic plague in Bombay: 1896-97*" T.O.I, (1898).

21. 47, Ghosh, Jayati – "*A critique of the Indian government's response to the COVID-19 pandemic.*" 519-530, J.I.B.E., (2020).

22. Gill CA.- "*Report on malaria in the Punjab during the year 1913 together with an account of the work of the Punjab Malaria Bureau*" S.G.P.P., (1914).

23. Geva-May, I. - Cultural theory: T*he neglected variable in the craft of policy analysis.* 243–265, J.C.P.A. (2002).

24. Gelfand, M. J.*et al. Differences between tight and loose cultures: A 33-nation study.* SCIENCE (2011).

25. Gaenslen, F. *Culture and decision making in China, Japan, Russia, and the United States.* WORLD POLITICS (1986).

26. G.O.C.- "*Rules regarding the measures to be adopted on the outbreak of cholera or appearance of small-pox: (G.O.C.C. No. 193 dated 3. Aug. 1870)*", S.G.P., (1870).

27. Goldin, Ian. "*The World After the Coronavirus.*" *Horizons:* pp 46-63, CIRSD, (September 10th, 2021, 9:00 am), https://www.cirsd.org/en/horizons/ horizons-summer-2021-issue-no-19/the-world-after-the-coronavirus.

28. Gostin LO. *COVID-19 reveals urgent need to strengthen the World Health Organization.* JAMA. (2020).

29. Habibi R, Burci GL, de Campos TC, Chirwa D, Cinà M, Dagron S, *et al. Do not violate the international health regulations during the COVID-19 outbreak.* LANCET (2020).

30. Habibi R, Burci GL, de Campos TC, Chirwa D, Cinà M, Dagron S, et al. *Do not violate the international health regulations during the COVID-19 outbreak.* LANCET (2020)

31. Hofstede, G., Hofstede, G. J., Minkov, M. (2010). Cultures and organizations: Software for the mind (3rd ed, 2010).

32. Hale, T., Angrist, N., Kira, B., Petherick, A., Phillips, T., Webster, S. - *Variation in government responses to Covid-19 Version 5.0.* O.U.P. (2020).

33. Hertwig, R., Grüne-Yanoff, T. - *Nudging and boosting: Steering or empowering good decisions.* P.P.S. (2017).

34. James SP. – “*Malarial fevers: A statement drawn up for the use of assistant surgeons, hospital assistants, and students.*” S.G.P.I, (1908).

35. James SP.- “*The causation and prevention of malarial fevers: A statement of the results of researches drawn up for the use of assistant surgeons, hospital assistants and students*”, S.G.P.,(1903).

36. Jessop, B. - *Redesigning the state, reorienting state power, and rethinking the state. In Leicht, K. T., Jenkins, J. C. (Eds.)*, pp. 41–61, H.O.P. (2010).

37. Katz, R., Vaught, A., Simmens, S. J. - *Local decision making for implementing social distancing in response to outbreaks.* P.H.R. (2016).

38. Keeler, J. T. S. - *Opening the window for reform: Mandates, crises, and extraordinary policy-making.* C.P.S. (1993)

39. Lyons RW, Childe LF. I. –” *Report by Surgeon-Major Lyons, I.M.S., President of the Plague Research Committee. II. - Report by Surgeon-Captain Childe, I.M.S. III. - Summary of work carried on by Mr. Hankin.*”, (1897).

40. Link BG and Phelan J. “*Social conditions as fundamental causes of disease*”. J.H.S.B (1995).

41. Markel H. Haven- “*When germs travel: 6 major epidemics of America*”Ny. P.B. (2004).

42. Migdal, J. S. et al. -*Comparative politics: Rationality, culture, and structure* 2nd ed., pp. 162–192. C.U.P. (2009).

43. Municipal Commissioner’s Office Bombay (India)- “*Report of the Municipal Commissioner on the plague in Bombay for the year ending 31st May 1899*” T.O.I., (1898).

44. Marjoribanks JL. – “*Report on certain features of malaria in the island of Salsette.*” G.C.P., (1913).

45. MacWatt RC. – “*Report on malaria in the Punjab during the year 1918 together with an account of the work of the Punjab Malaria Bureau*” S.G.P.P., (1919).

46. Mhasker KS. – "*Report of an investigation in regard to the prevalence of "stegomyia" and other mosquitoes in Karachi, and the measures necessary for their control.*" G.C.P., (1913).

47. Nomani, M. Z. M., and Faisal Sherwani. *"Security and safety of health care professionals during covid-19 pandemic in the context of epidemic diseases (amendment) ordinance, 2020.*" IJET 11.4 (2020): 23-26.

48. Nasir, K. M., Turner, B. S. - *Governing as gardening: Reflections on soft authoritarianism in Singapore.* (2013).

49. Nygren, K. G., Olofsson, A. - *Managing the COVID-19 pandemic through individual responsibility: The consequences of a world risk society and enhanced ethopolitics.* J.R.R. (2020).

50. Porwal and Acharya- "*A vulnerability index for the management of and response to the Covid-19 epidemic in India: An ecological study*", L.G.H., (2020).

51. Ross R.- "*Report on the cultivation of Protesoma, Labbe, in grey mosquitoes.*" S.G.P., (1898).

52. Sanitary Commissioner Madras (India: Presidency)- "*Report of cholera committee: ordered under G. O. no. 216 of 27th February 1867, to report upon the arrangements which should be made to give practical effect in the Madras Presidency to the recommendations and suggestions of the International Sanitary Conference*", G.B.;(1868).

53. Smith MJ, Silva DS. *Ethics for pandemics beyond influenza: Ebola, drug-resistant tuberculosis, and anticipating future ethical challenges in pandemic preparedness and response,* MONASH BIOETHICS REV. (2015).

54. Varshney- "*How has Indian federalism done? Studies in Indian Politics*", (2013).

55. Wollmann, H. *Local government reforms in Great Britain, Sweden, Germany and France: Between multi-function and single-purpose organisations.* L.G.S. (2010).

56. Yamin AE.- "*Transformative combinations: women's health and human rights.*" J.A.W.A, (1972).

57. Yan, B., Zhang, X., Wu, L., Zhu, H., & Chen, B. - *Why Do Countries Respond Differently to COVID-19? A Comparative Study of Sweden, China, France, and Japan.* A.R.P.A. (2020).

Online Sources

1. Altman LK- *Is this the pandemic?* NEW YORK TIMES, (June 8th, 2009) https://www.nytimes.com/2009/06/09/health/09docs.html.

2. Anjum R. Faisal, Anam. Sidra, Rahman. Sajjad –" *Novel Coronavirus disease 2019 (COVID-19): new challenges and new responsibilities in developing countries.*" NATIONAL LIBRARY OF MEDICINE (Sept. 10th 2021, 9:38 AM), https://www.ncbi.nlm.nih.gov/pmc/articles/PMC7644207.

3. Booth R. – "BAME groups hit harder by Covid-19 than white people", 2020. The Guardian, 2020. Available at: www.theguardian.com/world/2020/apr/07/bame-groups-hit-hardercovid-19-than-white-people-uk (Last accessed on May 20, 2022).

4. Chakravarty, I. – "As lakhs of migrant workers try to go home, Indian states spar over logistics: The Centre, meanwhile, has gone missing", 2020, Available at:- https://scroll.in/article/961566/as-lakhs-of-migrant-workers-try-to-go-home-indian-states-spar-over-logistics. (Last accessed on feb 4 2021).

5. Chokkakula- *"India's response to Covid-19 reflects the power, problems, potential of federalism",* I.E., (2020).

6. DW (2020)- "China cancels Lunar New Year events over deadly virus fears."2020. Available at: www.dw.com/en/china-cancels-lunar-new-year-events-over-deadly-virus-fears/a-52121516, (Last accessed on May 20, 2022).

7. Fleming A.- "Our face mask future: Do they really help beat flu, coronavirus and pollution? "2020. Available at: www.theguardian.com/ world/2020/jan/31/our-face-mask-

future-do-they-really-help-beat-flu-coronavirus-and-pollution (Last accessed on Mar 7 2022)

8. Gaby Galvin0 Western Countries View Covid 19 and the Spread of Infectious Diseases as Major Threat 2021 At:- https://morning consult.com/2021/06/10/global-health-covid-infectious-diseases-threat-poll/(Last accessed on Oct, 12, 2021)

9. Government of Punjab- Punjab Medical Manual- https://highcourtchd.gov. in/sub_pages/left_menu/Rules_orders/high_court_rules/vol-III-pdf/chap18part A.pdf (Last accessed on- Sept 7, 2021).

10. Howard, J – "To help stop coronavirus, everyone should be wearing face masks." The Guardian, 2020. Available at: www.theguardian.com/commentisfree/2020/apr/04/why-wear-a-mask-may-be-our-best-weapon-to-stop-coronavirus (Last accessed on Mar 20th 2022).

11. Kuznetsova, Lidia - *COVID-19: The World Community Expects the World Health Organization to Play a Stronger Leadership and Coordination Role in Pandemics Control,* FRONTIERS (Sept. 8, 2020) https://www.front iersin.org/articles/10.3389/fpubh.2020.00470/full.

12. National Institute of Health-"*Understanding emerging and re-emerging infectious diseases*" National Library of Medicine (Sept. 7, 2021, 10:40 pm) https://www.ncbi.nlm.nih.gov/books/NBK20370/.

13. Runciman D.- "Coronavirus has not suspended politics – it has revealed the nature of power", The Guardian, 2020. Available at: www.theguardian.com/commentisfree/2020/mar/27/coronavirus-politics-lockdown-hobbes (Last accessed on June 10th 2022).

14. Supplement to the Account of Plague Administration in the Bombay Presidency from September 1896 till MAY 1897, https://digital.nls.uk/indiapapers/browse/archive/74458388?mode=gallery_list&sn=1 (Last Accessed on Sept, 7, 2021).

15. Sandra C. Melvin. Et al- *The Role of Public Health in COVID-19 Emergency Response Efforts From a Rural Health*

Perspective. Centre for Disease Control and Prevention (July 23rd, 2017), https://www.cdc.gov/pcd/issues/2020/20_0256.htm.

16. Timeline of WHO's Response to Covid 19, https://www.who.int/news-room/detail/29-06-2020-covidtimeline (Last accessed Nov 10, 2021)
17. Townsend M. –"Surge in domestic violence during Covid-19 crisis." The Guardian, 2020. Available at: www.theguardian.com/society/2020/apr/12/domestic-violence-surges-seven-hundred-per-cent-uk-coronavirus (Last accessed on May 20, 2022).
18. Webster N.- American Dictionary of English, MERRIAM WEBSTER, (Sept. 7, 2021, 10:28 pm) https://www.merriam-webster.com/about-us/americas-first-dictionary.
19. World at Risk: Annual Report on Global Preparedness for Health Emergencies, Geneva, World Health Organization., https://reliefweb.int/report/world/world-risk-annual-report-global-preparedness-health-emergencies-global-preparedness?gclid=Cj0KCQjwlemWBhDUARIsAFp1rLXCjvZcX9NFAS9ysozSIWMQOwpqjIaiwa4f3xAI4Ni05bkuQBqmVJsaAkNSEALw_wcB, (Last accessed on 11th Oct. 2021, 2:30 pm).
20. WHO - Solidarity for Clinical Trials, https://www.who.int/emergencies/diseases/novel-coronavirus-2019/global-research-on-novel-coronavirus-2019-ncov/solidarity-clinical-trial-for-covid-19-treatments (last accessed on Nov 10, 2021)
21. WHO - Contingency Fund for Emergency - https://www.who.int/ emergencies/funding/contingency-fund-for-emergencies (last accessed on Nov 10, 2021)
22. WHO Timeline COVID 19, - https://www.who.int/news-room/detail/27-04-2020-who-timeline—covid-19 (Last accessed on Nov 10 2021)

LIST OF ABBREVIATIONS

AfFTA	African Free Trade Area
AGM	Annual General Meeting
AIR	All India Reporter
AJPA	Australian Journal of Policy Administration
AJPH	American Journal of Public Health
ALT	Alternative Law Journal
ART.	Article
AU	African Union
BBP	BanarasidasBhanot Press
BES	Bombay Education Society
BESP	Bombay Education Society Press
CARO	Companies Auditor Report Order
CDC&P	Centre for Disease Control and Prevention
CEO	Chief Executive Officer
CIRSD	Centre for International Relations and Sustainable Development
CRPC	Criminal Procedure Code

CUP	Cambridge University Press
D&CA	Drugs and Cosmetics Act
DM	Disaster Management
DMA	Disaster Management Act
DMJ	Dubai Medical Journal
DPSP	Directive Principles of State Policy
DRM	Disaster Risk Management
ECA	Essential Commodities Act
EDA	Epidemic Diseases Act
EDO	Epidemic Diseases Ordinance
EDRM	Emergency Disaster Risk Management
EGM	Extra Ordinary General Meeting
EIC	East India Company
FTA	Free Trade Area
FY	Financial Year
GCP	Government Central Press
GDP	Gross Domestic Product
GHD	Global Health Diplomacy
GMP	Government Municipal Press
GPH	Global Public Health

HC	High Court
HIV	Human Immuno Deficiency Virus
HLG	High Level Group
HOP	Handbook of Politics
ICESR	International Covenant on Economic, Social and Cultural Rights
IHR	International Health Regulations
IMS	Indian Military Service
IPC	Indian Penal Code
JAWA	Journal of American Women Association
JCPA	Journal of Comparitive Policy Analysis
JHSB	Journal of Health and Social Behavior
JIBE	Journal of Indian Business and Economy
JRR	Journal of Risk Research
MC&F	Ministry of Chemicals and Fertilizers
MCA	Ministry of Corporate Affairs
MDG	Millenium Development Goals
MoH	Ministry of Home
MoHFW	Ministry of Health and Family Welfare
MR&F	Ministry of Envrionment and Forests
MW&CD	Ministry of Women and Child Development

NCD	Non-convertible Debts
NEJM	New England Journal of Medicine
NHA	National Health Act
NI	Negotiable Instruments
NIH	National Institute of Health
NITI	National Institution for Transforming India
NS	Nudge Strategy
NY	New York
OECD	Organization for Economic Co-operation and Development
OUP	Oxford University Press
OxCGRT	Oxford Covid 19 Government Response Tracker
PAHO	Pan American Health Organization
PAN	Permanent Account Number
PM	Prime Minister
PPS	Perspectives on Public Service
PSLSA	Punjab State Legal Service Authority
RA	Revenue Recovery Act
RAMC	Royal Army Medical Corps
SARS	Severe Acute Respiratory Syndrome
SC	Supreme Court

SCC	Supreme Court Cases
SDG	Sustainable Development Goals
SEBI	Securities Exchange Board of India
SGP	Suprintendent Government Press
SGPI	Suprintendent Government Press of India
SGPP	State Government Punjab Press
SP	Suprintendent of Police
SR	Corporate Social Responsibility
TB	Tuber Closis
TOI	Times of India
UDHR	Universal Declaration of Human Rights
UHCI	Universal Health Coverage Initiative
UK	United Kingdom
UN	United Nations
UNECA	United Nations Economic Commission for Africa
UOI	Union of India
US	United States
USA	United States of America
UT	Union Territory
WHO	World Health Organization

About the Author

Dr. Deepti Meena is a highly accomplished author and educator with a strong background in public law. With over three years of teaching experience, she specializes in creating insightful research papers that have increased her university's visibility and students' learning. Her diverse skills encompass student progress monitoring, instructional technologies, curriculum development, and more.

Dr. Meena's academic identity includes numerous affiliations and academic achievements, such as her participation in various conferences and her publications in esteemed journals. Her educational journey includes a Ph.D. in Legal Dimensions of Public Health Law, an LLM in Trade and Investment Law from National Law University, Jodhpur, and a B.Sc. LL.B. (Hons.) from Gujarat National Law University, Gandhinagar.

Throughout her career, Dr. Meena has held roles as an Assistant Professor, Advocate at Rajasthan High Court, Legal Advisor, and Visiting Lecturer. Her roles have encompassed a wide range of responsibilities, from teaching and research to legal advising and representation.

With a strong commitment to her field and a dedication to continuous learning, Dr. Deepti Meena stands out as an influential figure in the legal domain, both as an author and an educator. Her work continues to contribute significantly to the advancement of public law in India.

ISBN : 978-81-965309-9-0

ASSOCIATED PUBLISHING HOUSE
BLOCK-77, SANJAY PLACE, AGRA-282 002
Ph.: 0562-4008061, +91-9897877556 | e-mail : vikram_jain2000@yahoo.com

Indian Pandemic Law : A Deep Dive Into COVID-19's Legal Impact
Dr. Deepti Meena
ASSOCIATED

www.ingramcontent.com/pod-product-compliance
Lightning Source LLC
LaVergne TN
LVHW012052160826
845678LV00014B/2799

* 9 7 8 8 1 9 6 5 3 0 9 9 0 *